of the extraordinary Jesuit have excited worldwide interest.

Readers of Teilhard who have felt the need for a book which brings together systematically Teilhard's themes and concepts will welcome Mr. Murray's introduction. Readers who want a general survey of Teilhard's thought before undertaking to read individual titles by him will find the clarity and organization of this book most helpful.

MICHAEL H. MURRAY was educated at Groton, Harvard, Johns Hopkins, and the Episcopal Theological School. Assistant Minister of All Saints Church, Worcester, Massachusetts, he was for ten years publisher and partner of *Editions Euros* in Paris. He has written extensively on art history and is the author of the novel *In Sight of Eden.*

THE THOUGHT OF TEILHARD DE CHARDIN

An Introduction

The Thought of Teilhard de Chardin

AN INTRODUCTION

MICHAEL H. MURRAY

The Seabury Press, New York

ACKNOWLEDGMENTS

Grateful appreciation is expressed to Harper & Row, publishers of the works of Teilhard de Chardin, for permission to quote copyrighted matter from the following titles:

> *The Phenomenon of Man.* Copyright 1955 by Editions du Seuil, Paris; English translation Copyright © 1959 by William Collins Sons & Co., Ltd., London, and Harper & Brothers, New York.
>
> *The Divine Milieu.* Copyright 1957 by Editions du Seuil, Paris; English translation Copyright © 1960 by William Collins Sons & Co., Ltd., London, and Harper & Brothers, New York.
>
> *Letters from a Traveller.* Copyright 1956 and 1957 by Bernard Grosset; English translation Copyright © 1962 by William Collins Sons & Co., Ltd., London, and Harper & Row, Publishers, Inc., New York.
>
> *The Future of Man.* Copyright 1959 by Editions du Seuil, Paris; English translation Copyright © 1964 by William Collins Sons & Co., Ltd., London, and Harper & Row, Inc., New York.
>
> *Hymn of the Universe.* Copyright © 1961 by Editions du Seuil; English translation Copyright © 1965 by William Collins Sons & Co., Ltd., London, and Harper & Row, Inc., New York.

Appreciation is also expressed to Helicon Press for permission to quote copyrighted matter from Claude Cuénot: *Teilhard de Chardin: A Biographical Study* (first published by Plon, Paris, 1958).

TO THE MEMORY OF
PIERRE TEILHARD DE CHARDIN

PREFATORY NOTE

I WISH TO ACKNOWLEDGE my gratitude to Father Robert T. Francoeur for his kindness in lending me manuscripts of Teilhard from his collection, and to the Reverend William J. Wolf for all his help and encouragement. Finally, I want to thank my wife for her patience and help in preparing this manuscript.

M.H.M.

CONTENTS

THE THOUGHT OF
TEILHARD DE CHARDIN
An Introduction

I rest not from my great task!
To open the Eternal Worlds, to open the immortal eyes
Of Man. . . .
I see the Past, Present and Future existing all at once
Before me. O Divine Spirit! sustain me on thy wings,
That I may awake Albion from his long and cold repose . . .
Striving with Systems to deliver individuals from those Sys-
    tems . . .
He who would see the Divinity must see him in his Children,
One first, in friendship and love, then a Divine Family, and
    then in the midst
Jesus will appear: so he who wishes to see a Vision, a perfect
    whole
Must see it in its Minute Particulars, Organized . . .
We live as One Man; for contracting our infinite senses
We behold multitude, or expanding, we behold as one,
As One Man all the Universal Family, and that One Man
We call Jesus the Christ; and he in us, and we in him.

WILLIAM BLAKE, "Jerusalem," *passim*.

Teilhard
and His Generation

MARIE-JOSEPH-PIERRE TEILHARD DE CHARDIN was born in 1881 to a family of pious, landed gentry of Sarcenat in the central mountainous province of Auvergne. He was born into a world hard for a twentieth-century American to imagine. The lines between tradition and progress—between the aristocracy, the Church, and the peasant, on the one hand, and the republican, the socialist, and the anticlerical, on the other—were sharply and bitterly drawn. Ever since 1789 the Church of Rome had stubbornly fought the republican movement with every weapon at its disposal and had found ample justification for its opposition in the excesses of the Revolution and of the more recent uprising of the Paris Commune of 1871. The triumph of the Ultramontanist over the Gallican wing of French Catholicism after the First Vatican Council moreover only widened the gulf which divided conservative Catholics from the intellectual and working classes, a split which is still far from healed today.

Ever since the condemnations of Copernicus and Galileo, Rome had resisted free enquiry in science, and the dispute over Darwin's theory was mounting during Teilhard's youth. An official warning against its unconditional acceptance was issued in the Encyclical *Humani Generis* as late as 1950. Meanwhile, science, increasingly isolated from theology, had been developing ever since Descartes toward the sterile positivism of a Laplace.

Such was the divided state of France when the defeat of Napoleon III in 1870 deposed her last Catholic sovereign, and the massacre and deportation of the "communards" both disposed of any Marxist threat and also ensured the sullen disassociation of the working class. The bourgeois republicans now engaged in mortal combat with the Catholic and monarchist conservatives during which time the Third Republic gradually took shape with the anticlericals in control, supported by virtually the entire intellectual elite of France, Littre, Renan, Taine, and Flaubert in the lead.[1]

In the year before Teilhard's birth, the Grévy government ordered the dissolution of the Jesuit order and of all religious teaching orders. The main conflict centered upon the schools, the large majority of which were run and supported by the Church.[2] Priests, monks, and nuns were expelled by the police and locked out of the schools; but the move was premature, for secular education was quite unprepared to take over the task. So official eyes were closed and the religious orders drifted back to their posts.

Rome and the hierarchy responded with meetings, pilgrimages, and anathemas in the spirit of *Syllabus Errorum*, while the government went so far as to forbid cabinet members to be seen in a church. In vain did progressive Catholics like Albert de Mun try to win the working classes to a mild form of Christian socialism. He and the priests who undertook similar missions were condemned, frustrated, and their publications were suppressed by Rome.

It was in this acrimonious atmosphere that Teilhard left the protected, private education of his home to enter the Jesuit college at Villefranche-sur-Saône. Claude Cuénot has assembled reminiscences of Teilhard's school days which show him to have been a reflective, independent, but well-disciplined student, already pursuing an intense private interest in nature, especially in rocks and minerals[3]—an early passion for what is hard, tangible, durable, and characteristic of his volcanic native province.[4]

In 1899 Teilhard entered the Jesuit novitiate, having stated his mission to "lead France back to God and make her Christian once more."[5] He took his first vows in 1901, just before the Combes government unleashed what proved to be the apogee of the anticlerical crusade, outlawing the Jesuit order and closing ten thousand church-staffed schools.[6] Teilhard, his classmates, and his superiors were obliged to flee to the island of Jersey in civilian dress—his first taste of exile.

In Jersey, he did his two years of philosophy, and at the same time made and published locally a geological study of the island. He was then sent to teach physics and chemistry at the Jesuit school in Cairo for three years. There he had his first experience of the East with its contrast between teeming masses and open desert, ancient splendors and present squalor. In 1908 he moved to Hastings, Sussex, for his four years of theology, and was ordained to the priesthood in 1911. While in England, Teilhard took part in several geological and fossil-hunting expeditions including the famous (or infamous) Piltdown diggings, and he made lifelong relationships with a number of British scientists and scholars in these fields.[7] He remained always an Anglophile, later extended to include many close American relationships. Much of his reading was in English, and he wrote and lectured fluently in that language.

As for Teilhard's theological training, many of his Roman Catholic critics are agreed that it took place during a low period when the late scholastic system of Suarez[8] was still the basis for Jesuit theology, and before the Neo-Thomist and biblical revival.

"In the Suaresian system, under which Teilhard was formed and against which he reacted, there is no inner link between human action and the divine gift of grace; the only link is an arbitrary decree of God," says Father Pierre Smulders.[9] It was a time when Catholic theology in general was on the defensive against any contamination from modernist and critical influences like that of Alfred Loisy, whose works were placed on the Index in 1903 and who was himself excommunicated in 1908. The traditional teaching was more devotional than historical or exegetical, and as insulated as possible from "worldly" concerns.[10] In *Comment je crois,* Teilhard himself writes, "Catholicism, at first appearance, disappointed me by its narrow picture of the world and by its incomprehension of the role of matter," and, he goes on to add, of history.[11]

It is remarkable, however, that Teilhard was given both freedom and encouragement to pursue his strictly scientific interests, and at the same time he received from his order a deep and solid foundation in the spiritual, ascetic life. The *Imitation of Christ* helped to forge his unswerving, self-giving devotion to his Lord, and the *Spiritual Exercises* of Saint Ignatius developed his powers of contemplation and imaginative intuition, as well as his missionary fervor, coming as they do from the Counter-Reformation period when the Church was most militantly concerned with every aspect of the world's material and historical life. Teilhard was to be a mystic all his life, but a mystic in the heroic, active, Baroque tradition which sought to explore, conquer, and consecrate the whole world to God, its Creator.

It was in England that Teilhard was first drawn into the controversies that raged over Darwin's, Lamarck's, Huxley's, and Spencer's various interpretations of evolution; but it was not until his study of Henri Bergson's *L'Evolution Créatrice,* and his return to France in 1912 where he took up biological studies under Marcelin Boule, that the evolutionary viewpoint came to permeate his whole way of thinking. In Paris he worked with Abbé Henri Breuil, discoverer of the Cro-Magnon cave culture of the Dordogne valley, and he formed an intimate and lifelong friendship with Edouard Le Roy, Bergsonian philosopher and scientist.

This happy interlude in Paris was soon cut short by the outbreak of the war which was to test severely and to temper definitively Teilhard's spiritual mettle. During four years as stretcher bearer on the most active sectors of the front and in the carnage around Verdun, Teilhard proved his heroic courage time and time again in saving men under heavy fire. He earned not only the admiration of his regiment, which cited him for the Legion of Honor after the armistice, but a *Croix de guerre* in 1915, and a *médaille militaire* in 1917.

The war, moreover, plunged Father Teilhard into the de-Christianized and Marxian world of the French working class, into intimate experience with brutality and death, and at the same time brought out the poetic faculty which remained strong throughout his life. In the midst of it all, he somehow found the time and the spirit to write essays whose titles alone show how far he had already gone in forming his mature, cosmic, and Christocentric synthesis: in 1916 *La vie cosmique, La maîtrise du monde et le Règne de Dieu, Le Christ dans la matière;* in 1917 *Le milieu mystique,* which later grew into *Le Milieu Divin* of 1926-27, and *L'Union créatrice.* In 1918 he wrote *L'Ame du monde, La grande monade, Mon univers,* and *Le prêtre;* the last, written in connection with taking his final vows of poverty, chastity, and obedience, is a statement of his mission to know the world to the full, share its loves and its sufferings, and at the same time, through sacrifice and renunciation, to collaborate in Christ's "divinisation of the forces of this world." [12]

In 1919, Teilhard was back in Paris to work on his thesis on the mammals of the Eocene in France, with work in the field near Reims, for which he received his doctorate with honors from the Sorbonne in 1922. Meanwhile he was teaching at the Institut Catholique, where his evolutionary ideas began to attract suspicion. It was at this time that he began a relationship with Maurice Blondel whose Christocentric theology of "Action" was strongly suspect for its "modernism." Teilhard also began a series of replies to Vialleton's attacks on evolutionary theory from the point of view of "orthodoxy." A crisis with his superiors was brewing, but the showdown was postponed when Teilhard accepted an invitation from Father Licent, S.J., to join him in Tientsin for geological explorations and the collection of fossils. Teilhard worked for a year and a half in China, making his first expedition to the Ordos region north of the Great Wall. It was here that, lacking bread and wine, Father Teilhard celebrated mass by offering all the world's labor and suffering to God in Christ, as he describes in his poetic *La messe sur le monde*.[13]

In 1924 he returned to Paris, to teaching at the College de France, and to his discussions with Edouard Le Roy, with whom he worked out his idea of the "Noosphere" of collective thought and communication. Le Roy's works at this time reflect much of Teilhard's thought, and they were to be put on the Index in 1931. The crisis for Teilhard, incipient since 1921, finally broke over the paper which he circulated privately and tentatively on the problem of original sin. It provoked a denunciation, and his superiors, prompted by Rome, ordered him to resign his post at the College and to return to China.[14] There he was to remain in virtual exile, with occasional trips home or expeditions abroad, from 1926 until the end of the Japanese occupation twenty years later.

In China, he set to work on his *Milieu Divin*, which he calls "a small treatise on the spiritual life," and he sent it with high hopes for its publication to Jesuit friends in Louvain. The two canonically required censors passed it "very favorably." But an anonymous reader sent his objections to Rome, and publication was forbidden.[15] For years Teilhard was kept in suspense, revisions were suggested and made, the work resubmitted, the answers delayed or ambiguous, but publication had to await the author's death. So began the lifelong trial of a man bursting with what he considered a vital, prophetic message to his generation and a crucial mission to a strife-torn world, yet forbidden to publish or teach anything outside of his strictly scientific specialty—an impossible assignment for one who passionately believed that science without Christ, or religion cut off from science, were equally incomplete and distorted.

The same fate awaited his more scientifically oriented *Phenomenon of Man,* for which he pleaded personally in Rome in 1948 after a careful revision to meet objections.[16] At the same time he was forbidden to accept the chair vacated by Henri Breuil at the College de France, for which Teilhard had been unanimously demanded.[17]

These bare bones of biography can give us little idea of the man, but may help us, as we go along, to see the formative influences and the early maturation of his thought in its historical context. For a living picture we must refer to *Letters from a Traveller* and to Cuénot's biography in which more of Teilhard's letters and essays are quoted in their life situation. But we must now pass quickly over the greater part of his life to note only what is of major importance to his developed thought.

In China, Teilhard became more and more intrigued with the question of the origins of man and of his relationship to the universe. Teilhard's part in the discovery and identification of the famous Sinanthropus skull [18] in 1929, in conjunction with American and Chinese scholars, was a turning point in his life. From then on he was called to Java, South Africa, London, or New York, wherever important finds, studies, or conferences on early man were in progress. He was in constant correspondence with French, English, American, Dutch, Swedish, and other scientists, and the theme of research pursued through international teamwork became a key image in his vision of man's future.

Long years of exile from his spiritual home threw him more than ever into association with scientists, most of them Protestant or agnostic, for intellectual companionship, and the ban on his treating theological questions forced him to address himself mainly to a scientific audience in language they could understand. With the approach of World War II, he came also to rely more and more upon American institutions to finance his work, and he became, as much as a man could be, a citizen of the world, familiar with every continent but Australia.

Completely cut off in Peking during the war, he had almost too much time, for one so active, for reflection and writing, until his return to France in 1946, when his hopes of publication were dashed once more, as we have seen. But there he had the opportunity to renew many old relationships as well as to form new ones, like his friendship with Sir Julian Huxley, then director of UNESCO, before pushing on to South Africa and to New York, which became his new and last house of exile until his death on Easter Day, 1955.[19]

The impression of spiritual depth and fortitude, of integrity, intelligence, humor, and disciplined passion which the man Teilhard made upon the many and diverse persons who knew him well is attested in recollections too numerous to mention here. Cuénot has incorporated many into his biography; others appear in a host of articles by Teilhard's friends and admirers.[20]

As to his unswerving loyalty to his Church and Order, despite tempters who urged him to follow modernists like Loisy into opposition and independence, his life is its own witness. We shall have more to say about the deeper significance of that loyalty and submission when we discuss his theology, but first we must outline as succinctly as possible Teilhard's central thesis from the side of science.

CHAPTER 1

World, Mind, and Spirit

"IF THIS BOOK IS TO BE properly understood," Teilhard states in his preface to *The Phenomenon of Man*,[1] "it must be read not as a work on metaphysics, still less as a sort of theological essay, but purely and simply as a scientific treatise. The title itself indicates that. This book deals with man *solely* as a phenomenon; but it also deals with the *whole* phenomenon of man."

The opening sentence above would appear somewhat disingenuous, for the book is plainly not "purely and simply a scientific treatise," unless we are willing to follow its author in enlarging very considerably the commonly accepted definition of science. He himself promptly warns us of this by pointing out that a science which desires to deal with phenomena *as a whole* is bound to involve a "complex of assumptions," an "aura of subjective interpretation," which carry it into the realm of a "hyperphysics," which he is nonetheless adamant to distinguish from a speculative, ontological, *meta*physics.

Useful as it might be to examine Teilhard's method before going further, it would be more in the spirit of his investigation to look hard at the phenomena as he presents them, before discussing his epistemology. One point, however, should be stressed from the start, namely, that when Teilhard speaks of the whole of a phenomenon, he means not only that aspect

9

which it presents to us today but its entire historical development, its whole life history, as it were, in time and space; so when he starts to describe the phenomenon of man, he starts, like the Bible, in the beginning.

THE EVOLUTION OF MATTER

"To push anything back into the past," Teilhard says, "is equivalent to reducing it to its simplest elements."[2] The most primitive state of matter-energy, the closest to a state of non-being which science can conceive of, is a near vacuum, a featureless and formless gas of similar particles. Such may have been the earliest describable state of our universe, for the original act of creation itself is beyond the ken of science.[3] But there must also have been present some organizing field or principle, complex forces of attraction under whose influence particles unite to form hydrogen atoms and the gas itself condenses into clouds, nebulae, stars.[4] There, under the influence of immense heat and pressure, a tiny fraction of this primitive matter is transformed into the heavier, more complex elements: the hundred-odd building blocks of all chemical substances.

Tens of billions of years and untold quantities of energy are consumed in this process, but under stellar conditions elements cannot combine into complex compounds. The next step can only take place when matter is either collected from dead stars or ejected from a sun to form planets. There a new process of synthesis takes place by which the tens of thousands of compounds are formed, and the whole planet undergoes its slow organization into barysphere, lithosphere, hydrosphere, and atmosphere. Thousands of millions of years are required for the emergence and granitization of the continents and to form all the delicate chemical combinations and equilibria which make an environment ripe for the appearance of life. Once again, only an infinitesimal fraction of planetary matter is transformed into the "improbable" structures prerequisite to life. Then, and not until then, was it possible for matter-energy to break through the next threshold from the ultra-complex and unstable mega-molecule to the self-sustaining, self-reproducing, unicellular organism.

We might pause here in Teilhard's description of the ascent of matter to look at the principles he infers from the phenomena described. Where science divides itself into physics, chemistry, and biology; and especially where astronomy, paleontology, and so on, are treated as special compartments within them; then the realm of each discipline is seen to have its own laws and characteristics, and the crucial thresholds between them tend to be neglected. What Teilhard has done is to join their domains along a temporal axis, and to look for the dynamic principles by which they emerge successively one from another.

The most evident of these is a dialectic movement, one of whose phases is the *union* of diverse elements on the same level—e.g., various sub-atomic particles to form atoms; the other phase being a movement toward *diversity*—e.g., the arrangement of carbon, hydrogen, and oxygen atoms into thousands of different kinds of molecules. The result of the two phases together is to produce many *new* entities which are both more complex and more centered than their constituent elements. This is what Teilhard calls the *Law of complexity-centricity*,[5] and we must clearly distinguish its products from the merely chaotic (non-centered) complexity found in an aggregate of dissimilar elements. *Centered* complexity is that which distinguishes a watch from a junk yard; every part functions in relation to a single whole. According to this principle, then, an amoeba is more complex-centered than a galaxy, and hence, on Teilhard's ascending time scale, of a higher order of being.

This brings us to the question of energy, vital to any dynamic process. According to physics, the universe contained a certain quantum of available energy at its inception, and it is this energy which impels the transformation of matter in certain local vortices of the cosmos from simple to highly complex states. Much energy is required for such synthetic transformations; only a tiny fraction results in the more complex arrangements, and these are relatively unstable. When they break down, some of their energy is returned to the system, but a certain fraction is irretrievably dissipated. This gives us the law of increasing entropy which predicts that the universe will "run down" as its available energy becomes fixed in "probable" states that are uniform, simple, and, of course, lifeless equilibrium. According to the law of entropy, our planet, man, and all his works are but froth and swirls in a turbulent stream in springtime, doomed to disappear eventually in a stagnant pond.[6]

This is the great obstacle to placing any final value on the products of ascending complexity. The law of entropy proves that cosmic history is irreversible, but, says Teilhard, there is also an irreversible countercurrent.[7]

THE EMERGENCE OF MIND

If physics is thus pessimistic about the final outcome of cosmic history, this is, Teilhard says, because it has only troubled to look at the world from without,[8] ignoring the presence of another kind of energy which is just as much a part of our direct experience as physical energy, namely, the psychic energy of living organisms.[9] This can be safely ignored in physics, but in biology it already becomes a factor to be reckoned with, and in human psychology it takes precedence over somatic metabolism. But the two kinds of energy have never been scientifically related because they appear to be incommensurable, thus engendering a fundamental dualism in man's whole body of knowledge. As long as this dichotomy in our thinking persists, no coherent picture of a cosmos which includes man is scientifically possible. Yet, at the same time, all scientific research is based on confidence in a coherent unity underlying all phenomena. Such a postulate is not itself an empirical observation; indeed, it contradicts our experience of multiplicity. Yet it has consistently guided science toward ever more fundamental and general formulations of the observed relationships between phenomena, and this has always been a criterion for the truth of scientific theories.

So we may say that Teilhard is scientifically justified in positing a fundamental relationship between physical and psychic energy and in then proceeding to search for evidence of their correlation. He finds this in the very process of ascending complexity and centricity which we have just described. By that dialectic, matter-energy rises from a state of simple, granular plurality, in which its movements appear to be wholly determined by the laws of probability governing huge numbers, through ever more "improbable" states of complexity, until, with the appearance of conscious life, its forms become so centered that they begin to show a certain purposive freedom and independence in relation to the deterministic forces around them. At each stage of this evolution—from particle to atom, atom to molecule, mega-molecule to living cell—matter, by its arrangements, crosses a threshold at which something appears which was imperceptible and unpredictable in the state from which it emerged. A *new quality* characterizes the complex and centered whole which cannot be explained by analyzing it back into its component parts, and yet which must have been a potential property of matter-energy from the start. Hence physics often loses sight of an essential quality when it attempts to explain or predict in terms of the lower anterior determinisms by analytical and statistical methods.

At the level of life, this newly emergent quality is consciousness, and as life itself produces ever more complex and centered forms, particularly in the development of the central nervous system and the brain, consciousness, as an empirically observed phenomenon, increases in intensity, quality, and freedom, until, in man, it becomes self-conscious, transcending the confines of the individual's time and immediate environment.

By observing this parallel development of the structural arrangement of matter and the rise of consciousness, Teilhard finds the empirical parameter by which matter and spirit, the "outside" and the "inside" of the stuff of the universe, are "functionally related . . . in a quasi-measurable articulation, with this double result, not only of furnishing us at last with a unified picture of the Universe, but of bursting the two barriers behind which man was beginning to think himself forever imprisoned, the magic circle of phenomenalism, and the infernal circle of egocentrism." [10] In other words, Teilhard believes he has found the link by which to heal the split between objective and subjective experience which has plagued man's thinking from the Greek philosophers to Descartes, Hume, and Kant.

The observation that spiritual and physical energy are the inner and outer aspects of the same universal stuff is fundamental to Teilhard's whole subsequent thought, and when worked out in the framework of his dynamic space-time continuum, its consequences are staggering to the traditional categories of both science and philosophy, not to mention, as yet, theology.

"The apparent restriction of the phenomenon of consciousness to the higher forms of life," Teilhard says, "has long served science as an excuse for eliminating it from its models of the universe." [11] But, he goes on to say, just as *every* mass is modified, however imperceptibly, by its velocity, just so *every* granule of matter-energy has two components, an "outside" and an "inside," the one vastly preponderant at levels of structural simplicity, the other emerging more and more at each threshold of complexity-centricity, until in man, the "inside," characterized by reflection, freedom, purpose, and love, comes to dominate and control, still within limits, the physical determinisms.[12]

The quality and energy we call consciousness, then, is coextensive with matter, and, moreover, like matter of which it is one aspect, it is basically granular and subject to the same quantum principle. Thus the determinisms, or rather the laws of probability, apply statistically to the vast numbers of simple entities whose "freedom" is infinitesimal, while *observable freedom* emerges by stages as the conscious component gains the upper hand through the synthesis of billions of granules into centered organisms. Statistical laws of probability remain valid to a modified extent, however, even in the realm of human history and social science where large numbers of individuals are involved.[13] There is, as we shall see, no sharp line between the physical sciences and a science of man.

The supreme theoretical consequence of this dynamic relationship between the ascending complexification of matter and the improvement of consciousness is that it gives us a scientific criterion of value.[14] As long as natural history was seen as a process of ramification only, producing by random mutation an ever increasing variety of forms, each existing for its own sake as it were, then science would be right in eschewing any anthropocentric hierarchy of values applied to its products. On the other hand, if evolution is viewed as the means by which consciousness, everywhere potential in matter, emerges and is transmuted into spirit, then natural history has a definite axis, direction, and, since we are now in the realm of mind, we can say, purpose.[15]

Having once postulated an "inner," proto-conscious aspect

of matter from the beginning, it is perfectly consistent to attribute the whole drift of the stuff of the universe toward complex arrangements and consciousness to a purposive, that is to say, to a teleological principle which works from within —not superimposed upon the laws of physics, but working through them.[16] In fact, such is the only rationally satisfying explanation for a process which began with a cloud of atoms and culminates in man. As Michael Polanyi has cogently demonstrated, random forces can indeed produce rationally recognizable patterns, but only in the presence of an organizing principle.[17] And in a letter quoted by Cuénot, Teilhard clearly states:

I am quite ready to admit your point that the extended play of large numbers can drive a portion of the Universe in the direction of the Impossible. But how explain that property of natural selection which *persistently* fosters the growth in the world of that *particular form* of the improbable which leads to those arrangements which are most organically centered and hence most conscious? Could it be by pure chance (as Bergson says in his *Creative Evolution*) that the *Weltstoff* appears to us scientifically as endowed with a special kind of "gravity" which causes it to fall, or rather to rise, taking advantage of every chance, by means of increasing its complexity, towards ever greater consciousness? In other words, if the *Weltstoff* was not "Loaded" [18] in a certain direction, do you believe that it could offer the least hold to a natural selection? [19]

Although the precise mechanisms of evolution are still hidden from view, Teilhard sees three activities involved: "groping"—a profusion of forms trying everything, and for the most part failing; constructive ingenuity—mutations and new organs creatively solving life's challenges; and indifference for what is not future and totality. All occurs as if random activity were shaped by a field of attraction which draws life's forms toward higher levels and future perfection.[20] Everything holds together "from above." [21]

Finally, the identification of the axis and direction of evolution toward higher consciousness restores the unity of our scientific and philosophical picture of the cosmos which was broken when man and his planet lost their privileged place at the spatial center of the universe. Since Galileo, our knowledge of the awesome dimensions of the universe, and of earth's infinitesimal and ex-centric (if there is a center) position in it, has made any anthropocentric cosmology seem utterly naïve. But the same cosmos, viewed dynamically, that is to say, historically, takes on a wholly different aspect, in which neither size[22] nor spatial position are of such importance as is man at the growing tip of the evolutionary axis— man, the most complex and conscious entity so far produced by the universe as a whole.[23] Physically small, but psychically the superlative result of all the synthetic labors of the stars, man is the spiritual, if not the spatial summit of the cosmos, the hope and instrument of its future consummation. Thus, in Teilhard's hands the theory of evolution, far from diminishing man by relating him to the apes, as so many churchmen used to fear, actually re-establishes him at the moving apex of time-space, well above the fixed central position which he lost in the Copernican revolution.[24]

THE EVOLUTION OF MANKIND

We have already paused long enough in our sketch of Teilhard's conception of our world's history in order to examine some of his basic theoretical principles. His imputation of evolution's direction to an "inner," teleologically oriented force contradicts the tenets of positivistic science,[25] but we shall have to return to this question in our critical examination of his method. Meanwhile, we must now complete our survey which will provide further illustrations of the same principles as they apply to the evolution of mankind.

As we have already noted, with the appearance of man,

consciousness became self-conscious and to some extent able to transcend space and time. Here we come to one of the basic problems of philosophy. What is the nature of man? What is his relation to animals, to nature? In answer, Teilhard points out that just as there was no absolute line of demarcation between the mega-molecule, the virus, and the living cell, so there is no absolute discontinuity between the animal's nervous system, the material support of its consciousness, and that of man.[26] On the other hand, just as a molecule of water has new properties quite unpredictable from those of its constituent atoms, so also the complex and centered arrangement of man's body and brain has surpassed a critical threshold at which there emerge qualities so novel as to carry him through a metamorphosis into a higher realm of being, incommensurable with what is lower. Yet the morphological leap is slight, so man is at once closely related to his animal ancestors and at the same time separated from them by a veritable chasm.[27]

With the advent of man at the growing tip of evolution, the "inside," which could hitherto only work gropingly through the play of statistical probabilities of physical activity, now begins to take conscious control of the process. Yet for the past thirty thousand years at the least, there is no evidence that man has advanced morphologically at all. Evolution on the somatic and cerebral level appears to have reached its structural limit as far as the individual is concerned.[28] The future of man does not seem to lie with some megacephalic superman. Is Homo sapiens as we know him the final and supreme product of evolution then? Has evolution ceased? On the basis of the principles we have described, Teilhard replies with a firm negative: evolution has not ceased. On the contrary, by entering a new phase, it is accelerating.

Every level reaches a limit of complexity.[29] The heavier atomic elements are unstable and transitory; the most complex molecules break down unless they are taken up into the realm of life; progress can only continue by periodic changes of state[30] in which the units of one level become component parts of higher entities. In man, morphological evolution on the individual level seems to have reached such a limit; but a new threshold is approaching, a new, critical, synthetic leap is in preparation.

At the beginning of each level, the phase of diversification takes precedence over that of convergence in the dialectical movement toward higher complex unity. So in the evolution of living forms the ramification of phyla, species, groups, etc. precedes convergence. Indeed in the animal kingdom, socialization is a late development in aging species.[31] In mankind's evolution too, ramification took place; early branches died out, and Homo sapiens divided into the several races, but these never separated into true branches incapable of cross-fertilization. Instead, five major ethnical and geographical foci of culture were formed, and, says Teilhard, ". . . the essential thing in history consists in the conflict and finally the gradual harmonization of these great psycho-somatic currents." [32] Not only does the transcendent dimension of human consciousness permit a much greater mutual understanding and sympathy, but the resultant development of a spoken and written means of communication provides the bond for the early convergent trend in mankind. So just as greater inner unity engenders greater consciousness, so the growth of consciousness favors sympathy between individuals, and fosters socialization.

A further consequence of the emergence of reflection and language is that the much debated transmission of acquired characteristics becomes overtly operative in the culture of human societies. Even if morphological evolution has ceased in the individual, the discovery, accumulation, and transmission of knowledge and skills from one generation to another, the amassing of resources, the perfection of tools and the means of communication, all contribute to the rise, both quantitative and qualitative, of the total expression of mind. It is quite possible that no living individual is the intellectual superior of Plato or Saint Augustine, but nowadays the *collective* knowledge and techniques of mankind are without doubt superior to those of antiquity. Heredity has, as it were, transferred its creative operations from the individual germ plasm to the collective sphere.[33] As at every stage in the ascent of matter-consciousness, the individual element finds its true function, the meaning of its existence, as part of a higher entity, through which it participates in a superior level of being. Has it not become a commonplace of psychology that the individual achieves the maximum development and fulfillment of his personality in proportion as he is both nourished by a richly endowed community and participates creatively in its culture? "No evolutionary future awaits man except in association with all other men," says Teilhard.[34]

So mankind begins by multiplying, splitting into diverse ethnic cultural groups, covering and conquering the earth. Within each group man develops innumerable specialized skills and varieties of knowledge; he thus completes the diversifying phase of his evolution. Then, and concurrently, the *convergent* stage begins. The pressure of population on earth's limited surface combined with the growing complexity of man's economic needs and technological achievements both demand and permit an ever closer interdependence. A global network of trade, communications, accumulation and exchange of knowledge, cooperative research, immixture of populations, and production of energy—all go into the weaving of the material support for a sphere of collective thought. In the field of science alone, no individual knows more than a tiny fraction of the sum of scientific knowledge, and each scientist is dependent not only for his education but for all his subse-

quent work on the traditions and resources which are the
collective possession of an entire international society composed of the living and the dead. Just as earth once covered
itself with a film of interdependent living organisms which we
call the biosphere, so mankind's combined achievements are
forming a global network of collective mind to which Teilhard as early as 1925 gave the name "Noosphere." [35]

Man's phase of diversification is far advanced, convergence
well begun; but, according to our dialectic, no critical, irreversible breakthrough to a new level can occur until complexification is completed by the organic centering of all the
diverse components of the noosphere into a unanimous whole,
"equivalent to a sort of super-consciousness." [36] But in a world
as far from unanimity, as filled with conflict, as our present
globe, have we any evidence that such a centering of the
noosphere upon itself will in fact occur?' Apart from the
trends already mentioned, there are unifying factors at work:
the breakdown of conflicting empires of colonialism, the
United Nations, instant communication, increasing literacy
and intercultural exchange; even the aftermath of wars and
the threat of atomic destruction shake the *status quo* and
force nations into closer contact and cooperation. Conflict
and the suppression of particularist forces is an inevitable
part of the process of unification. But all of these phenomena
together are not enough to guarantee the completion of a
centered noosphere. At this point Teilhard ceases to reason
inductively from observed phenomena and begins to deduce
their probable future manifestations by extrapolation on the
basis of the principles already inferred. This too is a common
and legitimate scientific procedure so long as the approximate
nature of such predictions is recognized and tested as new
data become available.

So, still within the realm of scientific thought, Teilhard returns to his original presupposition, that the cosmos is funda-

mentally one, and he notes that up to now it has produced a multiplicity of heterogeneous beings, interrelated to be sure, but also in conflict one with another. But, says Teilhard, if the cosmos is not to disperse itself into infinite and meaningless plurality, we must assume that the convergent movement toward unity in the form of spirit will continue to operate as it has in the past. An act of faith? Yes, but the same act of faith which underlies all scientific discovery,[37] and also, Teilhard stresses, an act necessary for our *survival* (the title he gives to Book Four of *The Phenomenon of Man*). For whatever becomes exceedingly complex *without* crossing the threshold to a new level by achieving centered unity inevitably disintegrates, a law as applicable to political history as to physics.

Mankind is thus faced with a major crisis, a matter of collective life or death. Until recently, evolution has pursued its ascending course automatically by the random and wasteful play of vast numbers in the field of a pervasive organizing principle. But with the emergence of self-conscious reflection and individual freedom, men became responsible for their own future development. Not that biological forces have ceased to work, but man is now free either to oppose and frustrate them, or to add his indispensable cooperation. Man must choose, responsibly.[38]

The pressure of population, the mounting resources in knowledge, energy, and technology, the "shrinking" of our planet—these are irreversible forces. If mankind does not unite freely, men will gradually be forced into totalitarian political union or driven to mutual extermination. But enforced union by exterior compulsion creates only a compressed aggregate of heterogeneous elements which de-personalizes them. The higher union in a complex-centered whole can be achieved only by a spontaneous inner force of attraction and cohesion.[39] This force of mutual attraction, which unites by the inner, spiritual form of energy, is love. Love, then, according to Teilhard, becomes a vital factor in a scientific picture of the universe. Like consciousness, it is not the exclusive property of living beings, but has its roots in the very energy which builds atoms and molecules into self-surpassing complexes. Proto-love, like proto-consciousness, is a universal property of all matter. It is the energy of synthesis whereby matter is raised from its lowest to its highest state. Love is the very motor of evolution, that second form of energy which carries the universal stuff in the opposite, and equally irreversible, direction from that of thermodynamic entropy, from "probable" states of plurality to the "improbable" but eternally stable state of total complex unity, by the integration of individuals into higher entities.[40]

On the principle that increasing complexity and centered unity support higher states of spiritual consciousness, moreover, the total unification of the world will liberate all of its potential spirit. Evolution will have succeeded in turning matter inside out as it were, transforming a full portion of its physical into spiritual energy, and its structural arrangements into that network of psychic functions we call personality. This is the goal and purpose of cosmic history and it gives us a "spiritual value of matter." [41]

But, and this is crucial, the "personality" which would emerge from the noosphere's centering upon itself is inconceivable, except by analogy, in terms of the level of individual personality known to us, just as the new qualities of each level of synthesis are unpredictable from those which precede it. Speaking as a scientist, Teilhard can only call it "*super*-consciousness" or "*hyper*-personality." [42] More commonly, he simply designates this "pole of convergence" by the symbol, Omega.

Having defined the goal as best we can in scientific terms, let us return to man's present situation. With man responsible now for his own future, evolution cannot continue without his willing and active cooperation, and this requires, first of all, that he know his proper goal. But, rooted as he is in ego-centric ambitions and local loyalties, man must also find the incentive necessary to motivate the efforts and sacrifices which progress toward unity requires. No impersonal ideal of the future welfare of mankind in the abstract has the power permanently to inspire the individual to shift his vital center out of himself in order to fix it in a hypothetical center of convergence. Nor is modern man likely to be attracted to the pantheistic mysticism which sees the individual's true destiny as a return to be swallowed up in an undifferentiated "ocean of being," for that is to deny the value of all the efforts and suffering, all the achievements, of the world's history as well as that of his own personality.

On the faith, then, that if evolution has a goal, and has conquered all obstacles thus far, it also provides the means and energy requisite to its fulfillment, Teilhard attributes to Omega those qualities which it must have if it is to be an *effective* as well as an ideal goal. For Omega to attract men's hopes, motivate their efforts, inspire them to sacrifice their egocentric individualism, Omega must be not only *personal,* but loving and lovable. The "It" must become a "Thou," to use Buber's expression. Moreover, Omega's attractive force must be actually present, not merely future and virtual; and finally, union with Omega must entail, not the suppression or diminution of individual personality, but, on the contrary, its expansion and fulfillment.[43] For, as Teilhard insists repeatedly, *union by love differentiates*. In the mass, whether in a primitive, pre-specialized culture or in an authoritarian, regimented nation, the individual is a more or less interchangeable unit. On the other hand, the more he participates in a complex and spontaneously loving community, the more he becomes his proper, distinctive self. Omega, then, is not an ocean of being in which the drops lose their identity, but a "center of centers," the focus which unites a new totality within which individual centers not only retain but extend their personalities in loving relationship to all the others through personal attachment to its supreme center.[44]

Finally, in order for men to have a firm and hopeful devotion to their goal, it must be capable of escaping from earth's inevitable death. Otherwise, all man's efforts and sacrifices are ultimately absurd and the whole cosmos is an abortion. But the very advance of evolution shows that Omega is *already at work*, radiating the necessary love-energy, attracting the elements into more perfect union, transcending time and space, just as human thought is able to do on a lesser scale.[45] When evolution has reached its term, when all that is capable of transformation into spirit has been gathered into a centered whole, then an ultimate change of state will occur: "the end of the world . . . detaching the mind, fulfilled at last, from its material matrix, so that it will henceforth rest with all its weight on God-Omega." [46]

At this point, Teilhard has evidently broken through the limit of scientific thought even by its broadest definition. But, as he says in the Preface to *The Phenomenon of Man*, "Like the meridians as they approach the poles, science, philosophy, and religion are bound to converge as they draw nearer to the whole."

We have already seen, throughout this first rapid tour of Teilhard's horizon, that a separation of his phenomenological observations and their theoretical interpretation is quite impossible within such a closely knit and universal system. We must make a survey of the whole, however unsatisfactory in detail, before discussing any one of its aspects in depth; for the object with which he deals is no less than everything that exists, has existed, and may yet exist, or rather, is the entire, unbroken, but developing existence of everything in a single time-space continuum. Like a well-knit symphony which exists as a whole, but must be experienced in time, no part of such a coherent complex can be understood without knowing the whole and that part's relation to it. Nor does Teilhard leave us any foothold outside his domain from which to evaluate it objectively. Many of Teilhard's statements appear to be quite paradoxical in terms of the classical categories of science and philosophy, and we must learn to adopt, at least provisionally, his frame of thought before these antinomies can be logically resolved. To do this, we must go on to examine his theological convictions to which his scientific train of thought has in fact already brought us.

CHAPTER 2

Christ and
the Cosmos

Let others perform their higher function of proclaiming the splendors of your pure Spirit! As for me, dominated as I am by a vocation rooted in the very fibres of my nature, I neither will nor can do other than speak of the countless extensions of your Being incarnate throughout matter.[1]

BEFORE EMBARKING ON an outline of Teilhard's theology, it is well to note that he makes no claim to being a professional theologian, much less a systematic one, but it is already quite apparent from our review of his scientific presentation that it has deep theological underpinnings and implications. So, leaving for a later chapter the question of the relative priority of his empirical investigations or his Christian convictions, let us sum up Teilhard's theological views as he presents them.

THE TRANSITION TO REVELATION

Actually, Teilhard has two manners of presentation, the one for the secular world, the other when he speaks "from faith to faith." But let us continue on the path we have already followed, which begins with man's experience of the world he lives in, which is also the one that Teilhard claims, in a number of autobiographical statements, to have followed himself.

27

"Never before," he says in a letter of 1937, "have I seen so clearly the possible significance of the evolution of my inner life; to begin with, the somber purple of Universal Matter transforming itself for me into the gold of Spirit, then into the white-hot incandescence of Personality, and finally (my present stage) into the immaterial (or rather supra-material) ardor of love." [2]

I believe that the Universe is an evolution.
I believe that the evolution is towards Spirit.
I believe that Spirit fulfills itself in a personal God.
I believe that the supreme personality is the Universal Christ.

Teilhard opens *Comment je crois* (1934) with these four credos, whose sequence is that of his phenomenological approach. We have already examined the first two terms and have been led up to the juncture between his "faith in the world" and his "love of God." [3] Let us now review, from a theological point of view, the final steps by which Teilhard's thought moved from science to religion.

Having described evolution so as to embrace the whole world process from atomic physics to human culture and society, Teilhard argues that if it is to continue along the same ascending line and by the same operative principles as in the past, the world's emerging spirit must not disperse itself and level off at the ceiling of individual human capacities. It must, on the contrary, take the next critical step in the synthetic dialectic of mounting complexity and centered unity which alone can carry it over a new threshold to a higher state of being that will free it from the irreversible decay of matter in its present condition.[4] But this vital step into centered unanimity can be accomplished only with man's free consent and active cooperation. It will demand effort and sacrifice, and ex-centration of his basic loyalties, and this cannot be expected, psychologically, unless an actual, concrete, loving and lovable, and hence personal, center of convergence is already present and at work. If no such person exists, then there is no ultimate hope. Man cannot give himself to "anonymous number." [5] The prophets of doom and of life's meaninglessness are right. Materialism cannot forever engage man's hopes and his best efforts in the face of an ever more regimented society tied to a dying planet. Hope, the motive of sacrificial effort, will die. Evolution will cease, and man, its crowning achievement, will perish with his planet. [6]

Rejecting the prospect of an abortion of the whole cosmic process as absurd, Teilhard says that man must look for a personal center of convergence and hope which will fulfill the requirements of his situation. And just such a person *does* in fact exist: the Logos incarnate in Jesus Christ, who has already passed through sacrificial death and who rose again as the universal Lord, who is present at the eucharistic heart of his body, the Church, and who is to come, "to unite all things in him, things in heaven and things on earth," "so that God may be all in all" (Eph. 1:10; I Cor. 15:28).

En pasi panta Theos was perhaps Teilhard's favorite citation from Scripture. [7] Three days before his death he wrote it on the last page of his Journal as the first of the three basic articles of his belief. [8] Thus, it appears as the final conclusion of his phenomenology and as the first article of his religious faith, and in the many essays which he addresses to the scientifically minded, he makes the connection between science (as expanded to include history, psychology, and sociology) and Christian theology at this point, that is, by tying them together at the end and completion of the world process.

A cursory reading of Teilhard's phenomenological essays might give the impression that he seeks to prove God's existence and define his attributes by purely rational and empirical means, as he himself remarks in a footnote to *The Future of Man*.[9] But in an important passage from *La vision du passé*[10] he says:

Just as the materialistic biologist thinks he has gotten rid of the soul in demonstrating the physico-chemical mechanisms in the living cell, so certain zoologists imagine that they have dispensed with the need for a First Cause because they have discovered a bit more of the general structure of his work.[11] It is time to put aside a problem so badly formulated. No scientific theory of evolution [Fr., *transformisme*] strictly speaking proves anything for or against God. It merely states the fact of a linked series in reality. It shows us an anatomy, not a final reason, of life. . . . The decision as to whether the course of evolution is intelligible by itself, or whether it demands a progressive and continuous creative act of a First Mover, is a question for metaphysics. Evolution [Fr., *transformisme*], one must keep repeating, does not impose any particular philosophy.

So if we examine Teilhard's argument more closely, we see that at least two other factors are involved in the transition from the evolution of phenomena culminating in Omega to the Christian belief in God. Science and history, as we have seen, can postulate the *desirability* of a personal center of convergence, and can even show the rational possibility of its advent (by analogy with the advent of life, for instance).[12] But they cannot *prove* its existence. For that we must turn to revelation, "a complementary source of knowledge,"[13] located supremely in the historical Jesus. If there is a real, active, personal center, it is only through the Church's witness to God's self-revelation in the incarnation of his Word that we can know him as such.[14]

For men to make the identification between the Omega of evolution and the Christ of the Church, something more than reason is necessary. A third factor enters in, namely man's existential anxiety before the threat of meaninglessness and the prospect of universal death, a threat which can be overcome only by an act of choice: *La grande option*[15] between a pessimistic determinism tied to the increasing entropy of matter, and the hope which rests on faith in a personal and immortal consummation of the world's emerging spirit in Christ.

Here Teilhard is making use of the same "method of correlation" by which Tillich sees revelation as the answer to man's existential questions and as providing an object of faith which satisfies his ultimate concern.[16] And so he ties three strands together in an eschatological knot—the empirical-objective, the existential-subjective, and the divinely given historic revelation which transcends and unites subject and object. But in the last analysis, the connection is made by faith, which rejects the absurd, but scientifically quite possible, death of man's universe in favor of trust in God's power to immortalize its emergent spirit by uniting it with himself in Christ: the faith expressed by Saint Paul in Phil. 1:6, "And I am sure that he who began a good work in you will bring it to completion at the day of Jesus Christ."

The one truly crucial contribution which modern science makes to theology, according to Teilhard, is to establish time rather than spatial or juridical relationships as the primary dimension for metaphysical thought.[17] This is the new Copernican revolution which forces us to rethink and restate all our cosmological, philosophical, and theological ideas. We must not only discard the "three-storied universe," but all the traditional fixed concepts of the nature of man, the relation of God to the world, of body to soul, of good and evil, the nature of the Church, and so forth, must be recast into a new dynamic framework.[18] For it is the attempt of traditional metaphysics to deal with fixed essences of things which is at the root of the paradoxes and antinomies of philosophy. In Teilhard's world, everything is in the process of becoming. Cosmology becomes cosmogenesis, anthropology, anthropogenesis, and even Christology, Christogenesis.[19] Only the direction is fixed and the full nature of things lies at the end, or rather in the whole completed process.

Teilhard's theological work, therefore, lies not in trying to change, add to, or subtract from the traditional content of Christian doctrine to which he held fast, but in the task of understanding it and restating it in terms of the convergent "Cone of Time," [20] and it is within this all-embracing context that we must trace Teilhard's translation of Christian doctrine.

CREATION AND PROVIDENCE

Whereas most systematic theologies leave the discussion of "last things" to the end, Teilhard (in his essays addressed to the scientific public) introduces his theology with eschatology. The reason for this may be partly apologetic, for it enables him to carry his readers thus far without explicit reference to revelation. But a deeper reason lies in his belief that the threads of experience, which now appear separate or at best parallel, will be fully united at the consummation of the world process. "When we turn towards the summit, towards the *totality* and the *future*," he says, "we cannot help engaging in religion." [21]

No synthetic process, in fact, can be understood except from the standpoint of its end. It is the *only* place to begin if we wish to see the functional relationships of all the disparate parts and the meaning of the various movements which eventually contribute to its completion. "Nothing in the world is really of value except what happens in the end." [22] Yet, from the time of the early myth-makers onward, men have sought to explain the relationships between the multitude of apparently conflicting phenomena by tracing them back to a common ground in the past. In pre-Hebraic mythology the best that could be done was to picture a primordial dualism between gods and chaos, spirit and matter, good and evil. The Hebrew Bible took over the myth form, but rejected its dualism by affirming that God created the world out of nothing and that disorder is the result of the creature's revolt against his Maker; but both the state of harmony and man's fall from it were still projected back into the time of the beginning. Until quite recently the story of Genesis has been widely accepted, not only as an image of God's timeless relationship to his creatures, but also as an authoritative and quasi-scientific account of man's natural origins. So theologians continued to search for evidence of God's nature and man's in the distant past, and to build doctrine on this basis.

Natural science has followed the same procedure in trying to explain all phenomena in terms of their antecedent causes. Both efforts are futile, Teilhard says, because in either case, tracing the world backward in time leads not toward unity or explanation but only toward ever greater plurality and formlessness until all things evaporate into the void.[23] "Contrary to the appearances still admitted by physics" (and we might add by certain schools of metaphysical theology), "the Great Stability is not at the bottom in the infra-elementary sphere, but at the top in the ultra-synthetic sphere." In other words, void and chaos at the base, and God in Christ at the apex, is the structure of the Cone of Time, with the "Prime Mover ahead." [24]

So God as Creator is best understood as "the God ahead of us" who is drawing all things out of non-being, over the thresholds of synthetic complexity by which spirit emerges from its material matrix toward final unity of love with himself, "gravitating," as Teilhard puts it, "against the tide of probability towards a divine focus of mind which draws it onward."[25]

One may well ask how such a view, which Teilhard him-

self calls an "inversion of cosmogony," [26] can possibly express
a Christian theology based on scripture by theologians who
never dreamed of Darwin's theory, who indeed calculated the
earth's age as a few thousands of years. The answer lies in
the fact that by the idea of the fall, the world was set back,
as it were, from its initial created state to a state of corruption coinciding with some indeterminate stage of its development as seen in evolutionary terms. In other words, from the
time of man's expulsion from Eden and the consequent dis-
ruption of nature's harmony, biblical history and evolutionary
theory can be thought to coincide. For the Bible, history is
the time and process required for the world's redemption from
corruption; so Teilhard's dynamic interpretation parallels
the Old Testament prophetic faith in God who has drawn and
constituted his people out of chaos and slavery in Egypt,
through the Red Sea waters and the wilderness, who continues to sustain Israel against the constant threat of backsliding into the raging waters and whirling dust—the symbols
of dispersion, chaos, and nonentity (e.g., Isa. 17:12f.;
29:1-8).

For Teilhard, too, the ultimate hope of biblical faith, that
which gives meaning to human history, lies not in the past
but in the future. "The divine presence in the Old Testament,"
says Jacob,[27] "may be defined as the presence of the God who
comes . . . [to] establish his kingship, an act that would not
be a mere restoration of the kingship he held in the beginning,
but which would be enriched by all the victories gained in the
course of history." Here we see the same pattern: in the past,
dispersion, conflict, insecurity, slavery, non-being; and also
God's promises and his power to fulfill them—events like
the Exodus which prefigure the end: in the future, freedom,
harmony, security, unity, with nature under the rule of man,
and mankind under the sovereignty of Yahweh (e.g., Isa.
11:1-9). The expected Messiah, under all his various pro-

phetic guises, was essentially Yahweh's agent in the establishment of his kingdom of the future, the new creation which was to transform the old.

Evolution, then, is "the expression of Creation in our experience of time and space," [28] and all purely scientific arguments as to whether "evolution" is creative or not are futile. There is little choice between the absurdities of the human spirit emerging by sheer chance on the one hand, and the creativity of "evolution" as an abstract noun on the other. In face of the claims of science, however, theologians tried to fill the gaps in the naturalistic account of evolution with special creative interventions of God, to account for the ascent of life to higher forms. But such a division of the field between science and theology succeeds only in destroying the basis for both.

For Teilhard, no such division is possible. God's creative activity is both continuous and in perfect accord with the principles of a comprehensive scientific method. Returning to his postulate of a "spiritual" inner aspect in all matter, and to his observation that science, once it reaches the level of biology, is obliged to admit a teleological as well as an antecedent causality, Teilhard argues that an inner teleological motivation pervades all matter, which, like consciousness, is not experimentally detectable below a certain level of complexity. It is, nevertheless, sufficiently operative there to carry even simple matter toward higher synthesis by "a sort of peculiar attraction which causes it ever to seize by preference, in the play of vast numbers in which it is involved, every occasion to become more complex and hence to achieve greater freedom." [29]

Therefore, God does not intervene from outside of nature, but works from within the very heart of things and through the material and psychic processes described by empirical science, adding, however, that essential motivation of purpose and the power of ascending synthesis which are inexplicable by a blind, mechanical determinism. God creates by uniting.

Addressing himself to God in Christ, in his *La messe sur le monde*,[30] Teilhard says:

Your hands . . . which do not merely touch here and there (as human hands must do) but which, immersed in the very depths, in the totality, past and present of all things, work upon us at once through what is most vast and what is inmost within us and around us. . . . Without shock, without thunder, the flame illumines everything from within. From the heart of the least atom right up to the energy of the most universal laws, it has invaded every element, every motivation, every linkage, of our cosmos, so naturally that one could easily think that it had blazed up spontaneously.

It is important that we dwell on this point because a great deal of what follows hangs upon it. Indeed most of the conflict between religion and science has arisen over the former's desire to allow room for God's creative activity in nature and the latter's need to defend the invariability of its natural laws.[31] By uniting the two into one continuous and coextensive principle of operation in which purposive spirit and the dynamic structure of matter work hand in glove, Teilhard provides the fundamental point of juncture between the new science and the new theology. He envisions them, not as dividing the field between them, but as letting each investigate the same series of phenomena, the one from the point of view of their empirically observed antecedents, the other from the standpoint of their movement by attraction toward a divinely revealed consummation; the one more apparent at the lower end of the ascending process, the other becoming dominant as the apex is approached. "Determinate *without,* and 'free' *within*"—a body's course is the resultant of the interaction of these two factors.[32]

An important example of the application of this principle

is Teilhard's treatment of the creation of man and of individual souls, a point at which evolutionary theory has been most attacked by traditional theologians who insist on maintaining a special divine intervention (e.g., the Encyclical *Humani Generis,* 1950). In paraphrase, his discussion in *La vision du passe* of 1949[33] runs: Many believe that only a miraculous break into the usual workings of the world can assure the superiority of spirit. But it is just because it is spirit that it must come as a crowning achievement. Every day a host of human souls are "created" in the process of development of the embryo in which no scientific observation can find any trace of discontinuity. . . . Why then make so much difficulty over the first man? As for the act of creation, the case of ontogenesis is the same as that of phylogenesis. Why not admit that the absolutely free and special act by which the Creator made humanity the crown of his work so influenced and prepared the world's course before man's appearance that man seems to us now as the natural fruit of life's development? Indeed, as Teilhard states[34] more briefly in *La messe sur le monde,* "It is impossible for a creature to be born other than from the stem of an age-long evolution."

If, by a literal interpretation of the myth of Genesis, Creation was completed with man's appearance, then its evident imperfections have to be accounted for by a fall from perfection. But in Teilhard's Time Cone, perfect union lies at the summit, and creation continues until that is achieved. Ever since man attained to relative self-determination and power over nature, moreover, he has become a co-worker with God in the creative process insofar as he cooperates, consciously or not, with God's purpose working within him and around him at both the biological and psychic levels. Thus, for Teilhard, creation, providence, redemption, and grace are all aspects of a single activity of God. The Cone culminates, you will recall, in the personal union of the individual elements of emergent spirit around a common center by the attractive force of love. Love is in fact the spiritual component of the energy which propels the whole process from the beginning against the tide of entropy through all the steps of synthesis toward complexity and union—proto-love, if you like, below the threshold of consciousness, but love nevertheless, operating within and between the myriad granules of pre-conscious matter, building molecules from atoms, organisms from molecules, until it bursts forth as the agape of Christianity.[35] And love, by its very nature, cannot be an external force, experimentally measurable, but is an inner, spontaneous force of attraction, working from center to center.[36]

Teilhard interprets quite literally Saint Paul's faith, "To those who love God, all things work together for good, to them who are called according to his purpose" (Rom. 8:28). But he so stresses the God of the future, his immanence in the world process, the emergence of spirit, and Omega as a goal, that he has been accused of holding the pantheist heresy, and of teaching either that God is, in his plenitude, the fruit of evolution, or that he is fulfilling himself through creating the world—views which are specifically condemned in *Humani Generis*.[37] We must go deeper into Teilhard's theology, his Christology in particular, before we can deal fully with this question, but we should already note the quite opposite view which he expresses in *La messe sur le monde*.[38]

In the beginning was the Word, regally capable of subjecting and forming all nascent matter. In the beginning, there was not cold and darkness, there was fire. There is the truth. So, far from the light's rising gradually out of our night, it is the pre-existent light which patiently and infallibly eliminates our darkness. We creatures, left to ourselves we are but shadow and void. You, my God, are the foundation and the stability of the eternal realm, without duration or space, in whom our Universe gradually emerges and fulfills itself. . . . [You are] the actual goal of a union a thousandfold more beautiful than the destructive fusion imagined by any pantheism.

Teilhard also warns us that when he speaks of the "God of Evolution," the "God of the Future," and of "Christogenesis" through human evolution, he speaks from *man's* point of view, from *within* the temporal process. "God, the Being eternal in himself, is, one might say, in process of formation *for us,* and God is also at the heart of everything." [39] So God is to be found not only in and beyond the objective world, not only at the end of time, but at the heart of man's being: "The deeper I descend into myself, the more I find God at the heart of my being." [40]

For Teilhard, God is not simply "out there" or "down within," but truly and gloriously omnipresent: "Incapable of identifying or confusing himself in any way with dependent beings which he supports, animates, and holds together, God is at the birth, the growth, and the goal of all things." [41] Moreover, since the Christian principle of union is love, it presupposes the real and permanent distinction between persons, who are united and differentiated at the same time. [42] "So is constituted that organic complex of God and World, the Pleroma whose mysterious reality we cannot call more beautiful than God alone, since God can do without the world. But neither can we believe it to be merely accessory without making Creation incomprehensible, Christ's passion absurd, and our own effort futile." [43]

We can go no further with Teilhard's theology of God and the world without first turning to his view of Christ and mankind, to which he has already led us.

INCARNATION AND REDEMPTION

Man, for Teilhard, is not a creation apart, but the finest fruit so far produced by natural evolution. And human history is a continuation of natural history raised to a more conscious and freer plane. We have already sketched his description of man's relation to the cosmos, but it would be well, before proceeding, to sum it up in five points.

1. Despite man's meager physical proportion in the universe, he is not only its crowning achievement, the bearer of its emerging spirit, but the spearhead of its future evolution.

2. Since the advent of Homo sapiens, the main ascending line of evolution has moved from the plane of biological struggle and heredity to the psychic level, from the individual to the social sphere.

3. Mankind, seen as an evolving community, is just emerging from infancy.

4. The next critical step (which may yet be a long way off) is the personalization, or rather, super-personalization, and immortalization of the world's spirit by the union of its "granules" by love around a universal center.

5. Man, as an increasingly free agent, may, and indeed must if the process is to reach its term, become a voluntary co-worker, responsible for his own evolution, in which case hope, born of knowledge and faith, becomes indispensable to the effort and sacrifice necessary to achieving the goal. The energy of mutual love attracting each individual center to the supreme center is equally indispensable.

It follows that any discussion involving a hypothetical fixed "nature" of man is bound to lead to untenable and contradictory conclusions. "Nothing," says Teilhard, "can be understood except by its history. 'Nature' is equivalent to 'becoming,' " [44] and this also applies to each human soul, tied to its particular position along the axis of the Time Cone. Indeed, each man is constituted by all that has gone before to make him what he is. The very elements in his body are products of history: its atoms built up by the stars billions of years ago, its cellular structure evolved in the primeval ocean, its anatomy the result of millions of years of struggle for survival. His basic skills trace back to the millennia during which primitive man's inventiveness gradually won its long, bitter combat to subdue nature to his needs. His ability to speak, read, and write, to educate his children; the moral law which permits him to live with confidence in society (one could extend the list indefinitely)—all of these are contained in the makeup of every normal individual, who thus sums up in himself the entire past of the cosmos.[45] Plato and Saint Augustine are still active in us, Teilhard says,[46] and this would be equally true of Nebuchadnezzar or Napoleon. On the other hand, even an Australian bushman who had never heard their names is nevertheless affected by the fact that such men have contributed irreversibly to the present state of the world into which he was born and raised.

So far Teilhard shares this view with behaviorist psychology and with the social sciences of man which are based upon biology, instinct, cultural and economic conditioning, and which (like Marxism) are usually opposed to the religious view of man. For Teilhard, however, it is only part of the picture, even if it is an indispensable part. Anterior and exterior causal factors, however integral to our understanding of things, cannot fully explain man's character.

Being is attenuated and finally evaporates altogether when we follow it ever deeper into the past. The importance of a river is appreciated at its estuary not at its source. Just so, the secret of man is not to be found in the bygone stages of his embryonic life (ontogenetic or phylogenetic) but in the spiritual nature of his soul. That soul, moreover, escapes a science whose method is to analyze things into their constituent elements and their physical antecedents. Only personal experience [Fr., *le sens intime*] and philosophic reflection can discover it. Those who . . . seek man's roots ever deeper and more numerous in the Earth . . . far from suppressing spirit, succeed only in mixing it like leaven throughout the world.[47]

Theology too, seeking to establish man's moral responsibility and to overcome the relativism which results from defining men in terms of their various ethnic and cultural histories, has traditionally traced man's nature and unity back to God's special creation of an original couple, that is, by way of myth. But even if we could return to that time, we would learn little from the brutish and barely articulate behavior of the first men that would enable us to understand man as he is today. The only way to understand the fullness of man's spiritual nature lies, not backward through all the ramifications which have led to his present complexity, but forward along the axis of convergence—in other words, to replace protology by eschatology as the locus of ultimate truth. For man, in conjunction with the whole cosmos which he crowns, is still in the process of being created. His true nature, therefore, is not in his past or present state, but in what his Creator intends for him to become. And that, as we have seen, lies beyond yet another critical threshold of ascending synthesis, in his union by love with all others in a new structure centered upon Christ-Omega.[48]

This means, first, that we cannot know man's true nature solely by empirical observation, and second, that the individual has no absolute abiding value in and for himself alone. He has eternal value, however, as the bearer of one unit of the world's precious, emerging spirit and as a potential contributor toward its final unity and immortalization in

Christ. It also follows that there is a limit to the degree of progress toward knowledge and socialization that can be motivated by biological and material factors. The Marxian, and other materialistic theories of history, would explain all of man's progress in these terms, but left to themselves they lead, in the long run, to the totalitarian ant hill in which the individual is submerged in the mass instead of being raised by union-in-love to a higher level of being. For in the complex structure of mankind, spirit has emerged to the point at which its freedom is potentially capable of dominating the physico-biological mechanisms which have brought it thus far, and if man is to progress beyond a primitive, materialistic, social organization toward a truly personal synthetic union, he must choose, freely and responsibly, to cooperate with God's creative work. "For the creature must work, if he wishes to be further created." [49]

In order for man to cooperate in his own further evolution he must, evidently, know what he is working toward, and we have shown that his true consummation cannot be fully known by a science or philosophy based on man's past or present state. Only God can reveal the goal of his creation, and without such a revelation, man would still be groping about in the dark (John 1:1-13). All progress would come to a halt at a certain level. But, at the very stage of history when such a revelation became necessary to furnish men with the knowledge and the love indispensable for their further cooperation in God's plan, Jesus Christ was born in Palestine—the creative Word of God made flesh manifested himself in history to dwell with men. The law, as Saint Paul so aptly put it, "was our pedagogue until Christ came . . . for . . . Christ has set us free" (Gal. 3:24 and 5:1).

At this point Teilhard seems to admit a truly supernatural intervention into the process whose natural workings he has been at such pains to keep inviolate. On the other hand, there is nothing arbitrary (except in the wider sense that the *whole* of creation is a perfectly free act of God) in the manifestation of God's Word, all along immanent in the world, in the person of Jesus.

The long ages which preceded the Nativity were not empty of Christ, but penetrated by his powerful influx. It is the shock of his conception which put the cosmic masses in motion and which directs the first currents of the biosphere. It is the preparation for his birth which accelerates the development of instinct and the flowering of thought on Earth. . . . It required no less than the terrible and anonymous labors of primitive man, the long beauty of Egypt and the restless expectation of Israel, the perfume long distilled by oriental mystics, and the ultra-refined wisdom of the Greeks in order that the Flower might finally burst forth on the stem of Jesse and the human race. All these preparations were cosmically and biologically necessary before Christ could set foot upon the human scene.[50]

The one real function of the world is the physical incorporation of the faithful into Christ who is God's. And this supreme work goes on with *the rigor and harmony of a natural evolution.* . . .

At the origin of this process, an operation of a transcendent order was necessary which grafted—in conformity with mysterious but physically ordered principles—the Person of a God into the Human Cosmos.[51]

[Furthermore] the determinisms . . . were so harmoniously directed and related to each other that the Supreme Transcendence seemed to spring fully from their immanence . . . and when the Virgin's time came, the final and gracious purpose of the universe was suddenly revealed.[51]

Teilhard must reach for poetic imagery in the few texts in which he deals explicitly with Christ's incarnation in Jesus. As a unique event, it cannot be subsumed under general laws or defined in everyday language. But it is "supernatural" only in the same sense that the first advent of life on earth, for instance, was "supernatural" in terms of all that was "natural" before its appearance. Both of these events were at once necessary steps in the one process of creation, and were also "new creations" born from the womb of the old without absolute discontinuity.

The time came when the Creative Word could no longer carry his work ahead through the physical and psychic determinisms alone. Even the divine law of Moses and the collective ideal of Israel had to be recapitulated and transformed into a focus of personal love in the prophetically awaited Messiah, Son of Man and Son of God. In order to unite to himself a world in which spirit in the form of *personhood* is the supreme value, God revealed his Word in the *Person* of Jesus, so that the goal could be seen to be, not an abstract collectivity, not some*thing,* but some*one,*[52] for in Christ, "the universe ahead of us assumes a face and a heart." [53] It becomes a "Thou."

Jesus came, therefore—to paraphrase Saint Paul—to free us by setting the attraction of personal love above the compulsion of law, that we might receive the Spirit by faith (Gal. 3-5). "When we were children, we were slaves to the elemental spirits of the universe. But when the time had fully come, God sent forth his Son, born of woman, born under the law, to redeem those who were under the law, so that we might receive adoption as sons." "Do we then overthrow the law by this faith? By no means! On the contrary we uphold the law" (Gal. 4:3ff. and Rom. 3:31). For love recapitulates and fulfills the law (Rom. 13:8; cf. Rom. 8:2 and 10:4).

For Teilhard, then, the incarnation in Jesus Christ is the emergence, in concrete personal form, of the Word who was all along immanent in the creative forces and laws of the universe (John 1:1-18; Rom. 1:19; Col. 1:15f.; Heb. 1:1f., 11:3),[54] which still continue their preparatory work below and outside the sphere of the Christian faith. The life of Jesus Christ is thus seen by Teilhard as a turning point in history, the culmination of all that came before and the inauguration of a new epoch of evolution toward love and personhood—the "Center of Time" as Professor Cullmann calls him in *Christ and Time*.[55] Yet Teilhard refers rarely in his writings to the Jesus of history and of the Synoptic Gospels. He seems to follow Saint Paul in preferring to know Christ no longer after the flesh (II Cor. 5:16). This is quite in keeping with his principle that the past can be fully understood only in relation to the end. The full significance of the Incarnation lies in its eschatological dimension. But we should not, for that reason, confuse Teilhard's attitude with that school of thought which sees only Christ's transcendent and eschatological value and hence depreciates both the historical Jesus and history itself. On the contrary, Teilhard insists:

This expansion [i.e., the universal Lordship of the Risen Christ] has value . . . only in so far as the light which seems to envelop all things radiates from an historical source and is transmitted along a clearly defined axis of tradition. The immense charm of the Divine Milieu owes, in the last analysis, all its concrete value to the divine-human contact revealed in the Epiphany of Jesus. Do away with the historical reality of Christ and the Divine omnipresence which inspires us becomes, like all the dreams of metaphysics, uncertain, vague, abstract, without tangible authority over our thinking, without moral imperatives for our life.[56]

So, having clearly affirmed the crucial necessity of the historical Jesus, Teilhard does not dwell there, but goes on to his "expansion" into the Cosmic Lord, the universal center and goal of convergence at the summit of creation.

In order to be alpha and omega, the Christ, without losing his concrete humanity, must become co-extensive with the physical immensities of Time and Space. In order to rule the Earth, he must give it a new quality of life [Fr., *sur-animer*].[57]

In him the Personal expands (or rather finds a center) until it becomes Universal.[58]

In other words, and here we reach the very heart of Teilhard's theology, the key to all that follows, the Incarnation is not a *fait accompli* on the first Christmas. For, "the Incarnation will not be complete until that chosen portion of the substance contained in every object, spiritualized a first time in our souls and again along with our souls in Jesus, has finally joined itself to the Center of its fulfillment." [59]

If we recall that, for Teilhard, all the successive arrangements of the matter and energies of the universe have been the matrix of its emergent spirit, manifest at last in humanity, and that humanity in turn has the function of gaining dominion over the earth, of cultivating and incorporating all that is of spiritual value in it and of carrying on its ascension and unification in Christ in order to offer all to God, then we will understand the cosmic dimensions Teilhard ascribes to Christ when he says:

The Incarnation is a renovation, a restoration of all the Forces and the Powers of the Universe: the Christ is the instrument, the Center, the Goal of the whole Creation, animate and material; by him was everything created, sanctified, made alive. That is the constant and continuing teaching of Saint John and Saint Paul (the most "cosmic" of scriptural writers) and a teaching enshrined in the most solemn phrases of our Liturgy.[60]

It should also be clear why Teilhard, like the New Testament, does not discuss the problems of classical Christology in terms of the fixed essences, universals, and "natures" of Greek philosophy and scholastic theology. It is, indeed, futile

to search his works for either modifications or elucidations of
the "hypostatic union" or the Chalcedonian formulae; for it
is no mere readjustment of terms, but the transformation of
the whole frame of reference which gives them their meaning
that Teilhard performs. This is the deeper reason for his apparent neglect of the traditional categories of Christology.
"Forced as we are out of the static Aristotelian cosmos . . .
we must re-think all our Christology in terms of Christogenesis . . . by the introduction of a new dimension (time):
a splendid task, by which, I can assure you, Christ emerges
veritably triumphant and savior of men's evolution." [61]

Nor does the "divine-human encounter" in Jesus raise any
uniquely difficult problem for Teilhard since, as we have
seen, "his immersion into the heart of the World" began with
time itself. And by seeing in Jesus Christ the personal em-
bodiment of the Logos whose activity is coextensive with that
of creation, and also a new beginning by which that activity is
raised to the level of personal love, Teilhard overcomes the
insoluble difficulties which result from attempts to explain the
nature and work of Christ primarily in terms of the brief
ministry and death of Jesus of Nazareth. On the other hand,
by expanding the concept of the Incarnation to cosmic dimensions, in time as well as space, he resolves the persistent
dualism between sacred and secular realms which results from
an exclusive devotion to a purely spiritual "Christ of Faith."

We cannot, plainly, pursue our discussion of the work of
Christ without taking the route of his passion and crucifixion.
But first we should again recall Teilhard's phenomenology in
which every critical step which matter-spirit takes over a
threshold to a higher level requires the expenditure of
prodigious energies (and suffering on the sentient levels), leading to a synthesis which can be achieved only by the sacrifice
on the part of the constituent elements of their individual
autonomy, by an act of ex-centration which unites them

around a common center to form a new being, higher on the spiritual ladder. Thus effort, suffering, sacrifice, and individual death are everywhere the price of irreversible, qualitative progress. They are universally necessary factors in creation (I Cor. 15:35-50; John 12:24f.).

The element must pass through the death of its old individuality in order to be raised, reborn, re-created. But, you may well say, Christ, the pre-existent Word of God, surely has no such need to pass through the stages by which creatures attain to their perfection. Christ is already that perfection, the image of their fulfillment, the bearer of the "new being," in Tillich's words. But, by his incarnation, by his "immersion into the great waters of matter" [62] sacramentally enacted by his baptism,[63] he voluntarily assumed the condition, the finitude, and the sin, of the world. In order to unite us to himself from within, he descended into our night, even into the infernal regions.[64] In Jesus, the man, the divine Word was revealed as a person, but was also concealed in the form of a servant, in which "he humbled himself and became obedient unto death, even death on a cross" (Phil. 2:5ff.). In order that Christ should be revealed as Lord of the universe, as the goal of convergence and agent of transformation of all things, he had to open the way by which all creatures whose condition he had assumed must pass on their road to perfection, the way of sacrificial love. So that men might be enabled to take up their cross and follow him willingly, he had to go ahead of them as a forerunner on their behalf, as the first-born from the dead among many brethren (Heb. 6:20; Col. 1:18; Rom. 8:29).

Here, then, is the key to the "Messianic Secret" and to the oft-supposed opposition between the Christ of the Synoptic Gospels and the Christ of the apostolic faith. The former were trying, within the limits investigated by the form critics, to present a pre-resurrection picture of Jesus, whereas it was only by his sacrificial death and by his resurrection and ascension that Christ was revealed in his full universal and eschatological dimensions which, for Paul and the Fourth Evangelist, overshadowed, while remaining an inseparable expansion of, Jesus' historical ministry.

We shall come to a fuller treatment of the significance of the cross and the resurrection when we discuss Teilhard's view of sin, the Christian life, the Eucharist, and the Parousia. Meanwhile we should press on to sketch the rest of the wider picture within which these elements find their true significance.

HISTORY AND THE CHURCH

"Christians," says Father Smulders, "are often tempted to see only half of history. From Abraham to Christ there was a progressive ascension towards Christ; after Christ there seems to be no further progress or ascension." [65] If, indeed, the redemption of the world was completed on the cross, as certain juridical interpretations of the Atonement would have it,[66] then the problem of the "time between the times," until Christ puts an end to it by his Parousia, is an acute one with which Paul himself apparently wrestled before arriving at his matured vision of the cosmic Christ (I and II Thess.). Indeed, all those who were close to Jesus seemed to have felt in his power the nearness of the end of which he was the revelation. But as the first generations of Christians passed, the intense historic expectation which characterized the people of the Bible began to be diluted and then almost swallowed up in the classical cosmos of fixed essences and distinct substances, and in the world of ideal legal relationships of Roman and feudal thought. Also, as Teilhard says:

The World's resistance to Good began to sap our faith in God's reign. A certain pessimism, reinforced perhaps by an exaggerated conception of the primeval fall, gave us to think that the World was evil and irredeemable. . . . Then we allowed the fire to subside in our sleeping hearts. No doubt we still pray and work consciously that "God's Kingdom come"; but, actually, how many a heart really beats faster in the crazy hope of our whole world's transformation? . . . To tell the truth, we must admit that we expect nothing of the kind. We must, at whatever cost, revive that flame . . . the desire and the hope for the great coming event.[67]

No, history has not come to a halt. Nor has it lost its sacred significance since Christ's ascension. On the contrary,

Everything continued to move onwards because Christ has not attained to his full estate. He has not yet gathered in the fringes of his Robe which the flesh and the love of his people furnish him. Christ's mystical body [Fr., *le Christ mystique*] has not reached its full growth, and likewise the cosmic Christ. The one and the other both *are* and are *becoming*.[68]

In this passage, Teilhard distinguishes, temporally, and identifies, eschatologically, the universal, cosmic Christ, and Christ in his mystical body, the Church. Meanwhile, each one has his distinctive yet complementary role in the world's evolution. The universal Christ continues, as before, to be active in all history, in the extension of knowledge and communication, in the progress of law, justice, and socialization, in everything that goes into the building up of the noosphere. But, as we have seen, in order for humanity to go beyond the structures of science and law into the region of personal love and knowledge of the goal of its efforts, in order for the noosphere to knit itself together around an immortal center, more is needed than can be achieved by cosmic forces working from below. The Person of Christ must work by attraction upon our freedom from ahead of us, and at the same time be present among us, radiating the power of love by which the whole process is carried forward.[69] "For God has done what the law, weakened by the flesh, could not do, sending his own Son in the likeness of sinful flesh" (Rom. 8:3).

And just as God's Word effected a long preparation for his Epiphany in Jesus, choosing, forming, and leading Israel as far as the law and the prophets could carry her, so he prepared mankind for its final transformation in union with himself, by the choosing of the Twelve[70] to be the core of a new Israel centered upon his own person, and by his continued presence and power in her sacraments. Within the universal operation of the cosmic Christ, a new phenomenon appears, the Christian Church, the ever-growing nucleus of the eschatological community, the pioneer of man's future evolution, "the consciously Christified portion of the world," as Teilhard calls it, "the central axis of universal convergence and the precise point of contact between the universe and (Christ) Omega." [71] Just as humanity is the growing edge of the world's evolution, just so is the Church the spearhead of humanity. In the Church the ultimate ideal of the loving union of all men in their common love of God is already realized. That is how she is able to unite all men above the conflicts of race, nationality, class, or condition. In the Church the essential and universal unity of the human family is already lived. What a contrast to the popular conception of the Church of Teilhard's time as a hidebound, conservative institution devoted to the defense of ancient values and worshiping a God from the past!

If Teilhard's description of the Church seems, even now, to be overoptimistic, we must remember that it is as prophetic as it is actual, that for Teilhard "is" equals "is becoming." He himself would be the first not only to admit, but to proclaim, as we have seen, that the Church, in its present, human dimension, has lost much of its sense of cosmic vocation and eschatological function; that it has even, at times, put itself in opposition to the progress of knowledge and socialization in the "secular" world. "Now I cannot escape the evidence that the time has come," he wrote to a friend, "when the true Christianity [Fr., *le sens chrétien*] must 'save the Christ' from the clergy (those at least who are the 'scribes' of the Church) if the world is to be saved." [72] But, whatever shortcomings he might see in the Church, medieval or actual, she remained for Teilhard the very axis and prefiguration of the new human society, indispensable to the fulfillment of its evolution, the only institution, as he said, capable of giving a living soul to the immense body of the universe. Although Teilhard hoped intensely for the convergence and eventual unity of the various Christian bodies (and of the non-Christian religions), he wrote, "I see in the Roman stem, taken as a whole, the only biological support both wide enough and comprehensive enough to operate and to support the expected transformation." [73] Teilhard, one might truly say, was more catholic than the Rome of his day, for he sees the Church as the Christ-centered community in which, and from which, radiates his life-giving love which gives to all history its ascensional power and direction, and also as the organ which gathers into one body everything of value produced by the world in order to offer it to God for its eventual transformation. For in each man, and in the noosphere, the material universe is already being transformed into spirit, and each man in turn contributes his share to the body of Christ by his incorporation into the Church (including, of course, the Communion of Saints). Thus, "the whole work, industrial, artistic, scientific, and moral, of the world, serves physically to build up the Body of Christ," [74] until, as the Epistle to the Ephesians puts it, "we all attain to the unity of the faith and of the knowledge of the Son of God, to mature manhood, to the measure of the stature of the fulness of Christ" (Eph. 4:11f.).

That is the epitome of Teilhard's whole theology of history and the relation of the Church to the world. But it can also be a point of misunderstanding if one separates Teilhard's secular activism from his Christocentric mysticism. The "vast quantity of goodness and beauty outside the Church," he says, "will come to fruition, no doubt, only in Christ." [75] And we should heed his own warning, "The work of the World does not consist in giving birth to some supreme reality within itself, but in fulfilling itself by union with a pre-existent Being." [76]

The City of God, then, for Teilhard, is not pursuing a divergent path from that of the earthly city, but rather, with Christ at its center, it is the spiritualizing nucleus of humanity and its noosphere, which in turn draws its substance from the still wider circle of the material universe. And this whole concentric system is moving within the Time Cone, with Christ at its apex, and the Church as the community which proclaims and prefigures the goal and whose sacraments provide the present animating and "amorizing" contact between humanity and Christ-Omega.

THE CONSUMMATION OF CREATION

We have now been brought round full circle to the end at which we began, to the keystone of Teilhard's theology, for it is there where history culminates that the significance and the role of each element becomes apparent.

Teilhard, we have seen, leads us to his vision of the end of history by two converging paths. In *The Phenomenon of Man* and similar essays, he tries to form an idea of the coming consummation by extrapolating the operative principles and ascending stages of phenomena as they appear to science and history. He describes it in terms of the organic centering of the noosphere upon itself, the "hominization" of mankind, that is, the emergence by synthesis of a unanimous, thinking, social organism which comprises and raises all sentient beings (on condition that they accept the requisite ex-centration of their egos) to a new spiritual level. But, he says, "The end of the world defies imagination." [77] Since it involves a transmutation of our very being to a qualitatively new plane, it cannot be adequately described in terms of our present experience any more than life itself can be described in terms of preorganic chemistry alone. "If Omega were only a remote and ideal focus destined to emerge at the end of time from the convergence of terrestrial consciousness, nothing could make it known to us in anticipation of this convergence." [78] Hence comes the necessity of the second path, that of revelation and the life of the Church. And it is here that the Christian in Teilhard has the advantage over the scientist, for it is to faith through the Church that the end is revealed in Christ as union with a person by love. But, since "we will all be changed" by that union, we can now know it but incompletely, and, as Paul said, we should "not pronounce judgment before the time, before the Lord comes, who will bring to light the things now hidden in darkness and will disclose the purposes of the heart" (I Cor. 4:5). It is not by experimentally verifiable knowledge but by the faith which gives us hope in things unseen that we are saved (Rom. 8:24).

So, without trying to paint an apocalyptic or millenarian picture of the time of the end, let us see just what we can, with confidence in God's self-revelation in Christ, already say, by analogy with things we know, about the consummation of history by Christ's Parousia.

To begin with, Teilhard says, we should put aside all traces of a widespread conception.

By habit, we continue to think of the Parousia . . . as a purely catastrophic event, that is to say, one which is apt to occur without any clear relationship to the actual state of Humanity, indiscriminately at any moment of history. Should we not rather admit, in conformity with our new scientific view of Humanity in process of evolution, that the spark of the Parousia will not flash, for physical and biological reasons, except between Heaven and a Humanity which has arrived, in its biological evolution, at a certain critical point of collective maturity.[79]

Humanity must first reach a point at which, "leaving the Earth and the stars behind it to the gradual extinction of their ebbing primordial energy," the earth's fully emerged spirit is ready "to join itself with Omega, the only irreversible essence of things," capable of delivering us from this body of death.[80] Not until then, Teilhard says, can the earth's "soul" detach itself without losing any of its achievements, as something fully ripe. The time is not yet. For, "have we any reason to believe that the human consciousness has already attained to such richness and perfection that it has nothing left to extract from its roots in the Earth?" [81] So just as Jesus was born in the "fulness of time" (Gal. 4:4) after ages of preparation, he will come to fulfill all time when all is ready. "As long as the fruit is growing and taking on color, we are careful not to pluck it."

As the end approaches, Teilhard believes, "a fearful spiritual pressure will be building up against the limits of Reality by souls in their desperate effort and desire to escape from the Earth." "Then the spark will fall and produce a brilliant explosion of thought." [82]

It is this intimate connection between the divine consummation and the progress of humanity which gives to history, in the last analysis, its sacred value. But we are once again led to the brink of a fatal misunderstanding. If it is man's efforts and achievements in building a more perfect and global civilization which will cause Christ to come and immortalize our work, then we are deep in the heresy of salvation by works. But Teilhard has already warned us of this. In the first place, we have seen that all of man's work itself, insofar as it is synthetic and hence ascensional, is in fact an expression of God's Word working through him from "below." [83] Secondly, man cannot ascend the final stages except by his conscious and loving faith in response to Christ's attraction from "above" and ahead. Thirdly, the maturation of the human noosphere is not the *cause,* but only the *precondition* for the Parousia.[84] "The more Humanity is united, conscious, and master of its energies, the more Creation becomes beautiful, the more its adoration is perfected, so much the more will Christ find for his mystic extensions a body worthy of resurrection." [85]

Finally, and conclusively, as we learn from Christ's passion and crucifixion, the ultimate transformation by which the world's spirit is immortalized requires that it pass through death before it can partake in Christ's resurrection and ascension.

In a convergent universe, every element finds its fulfilment, not directly in its own perfection, but in its incorporation into the unity of a superior pole of consciousness in which it can enter into communion with all the others. Its growth culminates in a transmutation in the other, in a self-giving ex-centration.[86]

"Our salvation is to be sought and attained only in complete conjunction with the whole elect community. There will be, in a certain sense, only a single man saved: the Christ, who recapitulates humanity." [87] Thus, "Christianity saves the essential aspiration of all mysticism: *to be united* (that is, to become the other *while remaining oneself*)." [88] For, "we, though many, are one body in Christ, and individually members one of another" (Rom. 12:5), "knit together in love" (Col. 2:2), and "if we have been united with him in a death like his, we shall certainly be united with him in a resurrection like his" (Rom. 6:5). "So it is with the resurrection of the dead, what is sown is perishable, what is raised is imperishable. . . . it

is sown a physical body, it is raised a spiritual body. . . .
Just as we have borne the image of the man of dust, we shall
also bear the image of the man of heaven. I tell you this,
brethren, flesh and blood cannot inherit the kingdom of God,
nor does the perishable inherit the imperishable. . . . But we
shall all be changed, in a moment, in the twinkling of an eye.
. . . for this perishable nature must put on the imperishable,
and the mortal put on immortality, then shall come to pass
the saying that is written: 'Death is swallowed up in victory' "
(I Cor. 15:42-54 passim; see also Phil. 1:6, 3:7-21 and Col.
3:4).

With his profoundly mystical and Pauline vision of the
Parousia and God's new creation, Teilhard ties all his threads
together and passes beyond the limits of what our language and
experience can describe. And this closes our initial outline
of his theology. But, having completed the circle in so brief
a space, we have passed by a number of important and controversial points which can better be discussed in the light
of our whole perspective. We shall return to these in the following section.

CHAPTER 3

The Christian Life

ON OUR FIRST TOUR OF Teilhard's theology we have looked almost exclusively at its cosmic, collective, and eschatological aspects. The life of the individual man or woman seems to count for very little in the perspective of billions of years of cosmic history, or even in the few millions which comprise the origins and development of our species. "It is a terrible thing to be born," Teilhard admits, "that is, to find oneself irrevocably and involuntarily carried away by a formidable torrent of energy which seems bent upon destroying whatever it engulfs." [1]

SALVATION, COLLECTIVE AND INDIVIDUAL

Splendid as Teilhard's vision of the "Cosmic Christ" may be, it is not easy for the "human molecule" to overcome his existential anxiety, or his individual sense of futility, by relating himself to anyone so grand and apparently distant. It is true that Teilhard's view of the Atonement and salvation is of the most "objective" type, but we shall see that he by no means neglects their application to the individual. He does, however, oppose those schools of theology which take their departure from the justification and sanctification of the individual, and in this he is again returning to Christianity's historic roots.

The Old Testament is essentially the story of God's creation of Israel, and of his relations with his whole people under the

Covenant. The salvation of the individual Israelite lay in belonging wholeheartedly to the people of God, and his fortunes, for better or worse, were tied to those of Israel or to her faithful remnant. Apparent exceptions to this rule are usually, on closer examination, elect individuals with a divine commission to the nation as a whole, and the patriarchs, Abraham and Jacob/Israel, for example, can be understood as collective figures like Adam/Man in Saint Paul's discussion in Romans 5 and I Cor. 15.[2]

Only with the political breakdown of Israel does a more individualistic note begin to creep in with the Book of Ezekiel and in the Wisdom literature with its Hellenistic elements. The Book of Job does raise, somewhat artificially, the problem of the semi-isolated individual's relation to God, but lacking an historical community setting, it is more a protest against a narrow moralism than a clear promise of salvation, more the expression of a crying need, than of new solution.

Daniel, however (the last book of the Old Testament in date), returns in this respect to the major theme by presenting salvation in the eschatological image of one like a son of man, the collective personification of the remnant of Israel, the saints of the Most High (Dan. 7). Like the Son of Man (Jesus' favored self-designation of his messianic role), the suffering Servant of God in Second Isaiah, whom the Early Church saw as an antetype of Christ, also appears to be a figure who embraces and represents the elect of Israel.

In such figures, then, and supremely in Jesus Christ, Son of Man and second Adam, the individual and collective aspects are fused into a single, supra-individual person. And Jesus, when all his disciples had denied or abandoned him at the time of his crucifixion, can be said to have summed up the whole of God's faithful people, past, present, and future, in himself alone,[3] so that in him they go through death to resurrection in a new body and a new age (I Cor. 15:20ff.; II Cor.

4:14; Col. 2). In the same way, Saint Paul understood baptism "into Christ" as an essential step in the salvation of the individual (Gal. 3:27; Rom. 6:3f.; Col. 2:12), and Irenaeus described the Atonement in terms of this "recapitulation" of all things in Christ.

Saint Paul did not on this account neglect the present life and problems of the individual, as the latter part of each of his epistles testifies, but he did put the collective, eschatological, Christocentric milieu first, as the indispensable framework for the understanding of the individual's situation and his redemption. The primacy of the Church's collective, historical role, however, was not indefinitely stressed in her teaching. We have already described the gradual erosion of the Church's sense of eschatological expectancy under the influence of Greek idealism and Roman legalism. Eschatology was even further divorced from human history by the secular pessimism which accompanied first the persecutions of the Church, then the decline of the Roman Imperium. The Augustinian split between sacred and profane history, the rise of monasticism and ascetic mysticism, and the growing conflict, in the Middle Ages, between a man's national identity and his membership in the Church, all contributed to an increasing stress upon man's individual relation to God, however much mediated by the Church. The concepts of the immortality of the soul and of individual judgment at death took precedence over incorporation into Christ and over the Last Judgment which would vindicate God's faithful people at the end of time. Justified souls, whether by faith or works, were thought to be collected one by one out of the world rather than as being saved along with it, in spite of Saint Paul's assurance that "God was in Christ reconciling the world to himself" (II Cor. 5:19; cf. John 3:16f., 12:47).[4]

The Church has, of course, always kept its apostolic heritage alive in its Scriptures, Creeds, liturgy, and classic theologians.

But it has too often allowed the cosmic dimensions of its theology to remain in the background or to be appended as a postscript to its more immediate concerns. This trend toward individualism not only contributed to the shattering of Christ's body on earth in the Reformation, but was also carried to new extremes in some Protestant sects.

It was particularly strong in the nineteenth-century atmosphere of liberal, humanistic individualism on the one hand, and of Catholic defensive warfare against secular progressivism on the other. It has been said that all major movements for reform go back to Paul, and Teilhard, on the Catholic side, is one of the foremost pioneers in the present trend to restore the Pauline, cosmic, historical, and eschatological framework, that is to say, of the whole picture of God's plan for the world's salvation to its rightful and necessary primacy in Christian theology. On this ground, the reconciliation of the world to God in Christ can proceed with man's full participation, and it is through mutual cooperation in this effort, as their primary and God-given duty, that the divided churches can converge around their common Lord.[5]

CHRIST AND THE INDIVIDUAL

Every man is a creature of God produced by an age-long evolution in which he is deeply rooted and inextricably involved, body and soul. The individual man or woman cannot therefore, in Teilhard's perspective, be abstracted from his or her position in the world of time to be defined and judged *sub specie aeternitatis*. Each one is what he is at any given moment *because* of his unique position, spatial and temporal, both in the history of the cosmos and in the course of his own individual development. So we cannot speak of what is right or wrong for any individual until we can place him in relation to the process which produced him and to which he is destined to contribute.[6]

One of the principles of the biological process which brought man to the threshold of social consciousness was that of indifference for the individual units which, in the struggle for survival of the fittest, were sacrificed for the improvement of the phylum.[7] But as man matures, another principle grows up alongside the first. The future of evolution no longer lies in the improvement of select individuals at the expense of others, for, "In this perspective, Life, having arrived at the level of reflection, would not only disperse itself into divergent ethno-cultural groups, but would culminate (and one might say, evaporate) in isolated individuals, each . . . representing a separate and absolute summit of the universe." [8] This is a dead end. But in human society, convergence begins to replace divergence, and cooperation to prevail over competition.

The creative Word of God, working from below through psycho-biological forces (including human reason), and from outside the individual through geographic, sociological factors, guides and impels mankind toward greater unity, legal justice, and the construction of the noosphere. Even the infidels and agnostics collaborate unconsciously and involuntarily toward the kingdom of God, Teilhard says,[9] but this is only a temporary phase in the world's evolution. There is a limit to how far the Word, working through universal forces from below, can carry man without his conscious, faithful, and willing cooperation.

In order to progress beyond a society which attempts to harmonize men's competing needs and ambitions by an increasing reliance on depersonalized law and force, it is necessary that men respond to the higher level of Christ's activity which works by attraction from above and by love from within the individual.

As in society, so in the individual; there is a limit to how far his "natural" endowment can carry him. Without faith in something higher than himself, his spirit is trapped in the small circle of his self-satisfaction whose future is blocked by age, illness, the competition of others, and death. Even if he places his faith in the aggregate of his human community, he will be giving himself to something less than the *person* he already is himself; to something from which he will be severed by his own death; and to something whose future, without faith in Christ, can only bring still further depersonalizing regimentation until the earth ends in total death.

For the man who sees nothing higher than himself at the end of World History, daily life is full of trivia and vexation. How many futile efforts! How much wasted time! But for those who see the synthesis of spirit proceeding beyond their brief existence, every action and every event becomes charged with interest and promise.[10]

Man's mind, says Teilhard, "is essentially the power of synthesis and organization,"[11] and the attainment to more being is the achievement of more unity of complex elements.[12] So a man, if he is to ascend to higher consciousness and greater being, must be ever enlarging the sphere of his interests, the network of his relationships and activities, the radius of his person, and at the same time he must be integrating all his inner functions around a common center. Expansion and complexification on the one hand, and centered unity on the other must grow together in the developing individual, who "cannot fulfil himself, that is, become fully conscious and personal, except in solidarity with all other men, present, past, and future."[13] In other words, for a man to integrate himself, to call forth his best efforts, to find clear meaning and purpose for his life, to grow to the full capacities of his spiritual being, he must relate himself as a part to the whole, and that entails moving the normative center of his being out of himself and attaching it to the center of totality.[14] But, since it is a contradiction in terms to move a center out of its own sphere, this also entails taking the center of totality into the center of a man's own being. Furthermore, this center, if it is to be worthy of a man's love and capable of being taken into the center of his self, cannot be an abstraction, nor of a lower order than the personal and spiritual center man already has. Christ alone, of everything we know, is at the same time personal (or rather supra-personal) and also comprehends the totality of things both as agent of their creation and as the term of their convergent unity. And Christ, by his incarnation in Jesus, through his Church and sacraments, also offers to enter and to work within the faithful individual.

It follows that man cannot become what he is destined to be without encountering Christ and believing in him. But man, as he is today, is still a creature in transition, not yet mature. He is torn, within himself, between the old psycho-biological drives toward individuation and competition which have served to bring him thus far, and the newer demands of his emerging spirit striving toward the future and totality. For Teilhard, as for Saint Paul, the physical comes first (in time) and then the spiritual (I Cor. 15:46). So each man must first become a distinct and responsible self, before he can extend his personality or give himself in love to another. "Our own soul . . . is the first of the tasks calling for our efforts," Teilhard wrote to a friend.[15] Indeed, unlike the animal whose major instinctual end is the reproduction of the species, man tends to live for himself alone. The emergence of reflective self-consciousness entails self-centeredness as a necessary first step.[16] But egoism also becomes the great obstacle to further progress. "In trying to separate itself as much as possible from others, the element individualizes itself; but in doing so it becomes retrograde and seeks to drag the world backwards towards plurality and into matter." [17] Is this not the essence of original sin which appeared for the first time with man's autonomous self-consciousness—the *felix culpa* which can be overcome only by raising that consciousness to a still higher level by the individual's recentering of himself in Christ?

Man's fatal mistake, says Teilhard, "is to confuse individuality with personality." We can only be fully ourselves, find our true person, by uniting with others. "The true ego grows in inverse proportion to egoism." [18]

Love alone, as we have already seen, is able to unite men in such a way as to amplify and fulfill the person of each; but, "man's capacity, it may seem, is confined to giving his affection to one human being or to very few. Beyond that radius the heart does not carry, and there is only room for cold justice and cold reason." [19] Because of his original sin—quite literally the sin inherent in the origin of his egocentric self-consciousness[20]—man, even at his best, if left to himself, quickly reaches the intrinsic limit of his self-development. The apparent impossibility of going further without losing his most precious possession, his very selfhood, blocks his view of any future issue by which his spirit can transcend the limits imposed by its matrix of flesh.

So egoism, internal division, anxiety for the future, and fear of death are the inherent maladies of natural man, and it is from these that Christ came to cure him. Natural man is enslaved to the psycho-biological forces by means of which he was brought into being, and it is from these powers that Christ came to liberate him. By submitting himself to the law of the flesh, and on the cross overcoming it by the power of sacrificial love, Christ objectively set in motion a new force, a new epoch of evolution, which is to culminate in the unity of love. This is Christ's work of At-one-ment. At the same time he defeated the lower powers of the world, not by condemning and rejecting them, but in the far greater victory of harnessing their energies for his purpose, "leading them in triumphal procession upon the cross" (Col. 2:15).[21] Since Christ's death and resurrection, law is subservient to love as the supreme, guiding, and energizing force in the universe.

Christ's redemptive work is not objective only. Salvation, in cosmic terms, is an eschatological event, the fruit of the union of all the faithful with Christ at his Parousia; but each individual who meets Christ and believes in him is saved here and now by faith in him who provides the hope and radiates the love which is lacking for each man to make the act of ex-centration that opens the way to his own fulfillment as a person. Faith in Christ-Omega, says Teilhard, has the effect of breaking "the infernal circle of ego-centrism, what might be called our ontological isolation, which prevents each one of us from coming out of our selves to enter into the point of view of even those we most love: as if the universe as a whole were composed of as many mutually repellent sub-universes as there were self-centered conscious beings. . . . Who can trace the long chain of evil consequences brought about by this atomic point of view? . . . Iron laws of economics, the invincible resurgence of nationalisms, the apparent inevitability of wars . . . ?" But faith changes all that: "It is a whole new world of relationships which begins." [22] Faith changes a man so radically that by it he is made a new creation in Christ; he is transferred from the former age of divergence, isolation, and stagnation, to the new age of convergence in love, "living no longer for himself but for him who for his sake died and was raised" (II Cor. 4:15f.): "set free from the law of sin and death" (Rom. 8:2).

But natural man, enslaved as he is to the law of the flesh, cannot attain to faith by himself. Faith is a gift of God, not of man's own devising. He can receive it only in gratitude, not with pride in his own merit.[23] He is nevertheless free to accept or reject God's gift. "We ourselves save or lose ourselves," Teilhard insists. "This Christian dogma of individual salvation ✓

is all the more necessary to stress as the context we are developing is more collective and universal." [24] Each man must choose between the dead end of egocentric individualism rooted in the natural but inferior forces of his past evolution, and the Christocentric love which alone can carry him over the threshold to larger life. This choice is not, as a "fixist" ideal metaphysics would have it, an abrupt and exclusive one between Christ and spirit on the one hand and the world and flesh on the other. The choice is a profound and decisive one which alters one's very being, but it is at first an invisible reorientation, the beginning of a dynamic process. In the world at large, it makes all the difference whether it is in process of an evolution guided and impelled from ahead or whether it is merely a kind of self-sustaining cycle of change and decay, and yet neither the fact nor the direction of its evolution can be detected without reference to an extremely long period of its history. Just so, in the individual, the subjective effect of his incorporation by baptism and his justification by faith is an illumination and reorientation of the very core of his being which need cause no immediately detectable transformation of his personality. Christ's work through faith within the individual, like his work in the cosmos, operates through the existing psycho-biological structures by becoming their directing and organizing principle, and is hence outwardly indistinguishable from the operation of human reason, emotions, and bodily activity of natural man, except by the direction of their growth. By their fruits you shall know them. The whole is known by its end, and if it is healthy, if it is "saved," it will be shaped from the time of its new beginning by its end.

This brings us to a major theme of Teilhard's view of the Christian life in its mystical and ethical aspects. Teilhard repeatedly rejects the "other worldly" strain in Christian piety and mysticism, which he considers to be an orientalizing adulteration of the true "occidental" (i.e., Judaeo-Christian) mysticism.[25] "There are at present," he says, "two opposed Christianities, a Christianity which disdains the world (the way of escape) and a Christianity which overcomes (the way of evolution).[26]

One text so well sums up Teilhard's thesis and ties it to all that has gone before that I quote it at length:

Whoever believes in Heaven comes to realize that the mystical transformation for which he so ardently hopes presupposes and consecrates all the tangible realities and all the laborious stages of human progress. In order to be supra-spiritualized in God must not Humanity be first of all born and raised up in conformity with the whole process we call evolution? If so, it means for the Christian in particular, a radical incorporation of terrestrial values into the most fundamental tenets of his faith; that of Divine Omnipotence first of all. God creates us and works upon us through evolution: how can we imagine or fear that he can interfere arbitrarily with the very process by which his activity is expressed? And again in our notion of detachment: God awaits us as the culmination of evolution; to overcome the World, then, does not mean to scorn or reject it, but to traverse it and to sublimate it. Of love, finally: the Love of God expresses and crowns the deep affinity which, since the dawn of Time, and Space, gathers and concentrates the spiritualizable elements of the Universe. To love God and one's neighbor, therefore, is not a mere act of veneration and pity superimposed upon our individual preoccupations. It is Life itself.[27]

INDIVIDUAL CHRISTIAN EVOLUTION

For Teilhard, the individual is not only a product of divine evolution, he is not only caught up in the current of cosmic evolution, his own inner life is itself an evolution: an evolution which, as we have seen, can proceed just so far by virtue of its natural endowment, and which requires the conscious choice of faith and loving adhesion to Christ to complete,

consummate, and immortalize it. But an evolution takes time
and proceeds by stages. Our own soul, which, as Teilhard said,
is the first task calling for our effort, is not something given us
apart from our body, but is "inseparable, in its birth and
growth, from the universe in which it is born and which it
sums up in a particular way." Nor is it given to us fully fash-
ioned. "It is we ourselves, by our activity, who must assemble
its elements scattered everywhere" in the universe which it is
designed to incorporate and to spiritualize in its conscious life.
"Thus every man . . . constructs his own soul throughout his
life on earth[28] and at the same time he collaborates in another
work . . . which infinitely surpasses it . . . , the completion of the world. [For] by the spiritualizing efforts of individuals [the world] gradually accumulates out of all matter that
which will make it over into the heavenly Jerusalem, the new
Earth." [29]

Each man is inserted at a particular point in the great Cone
of time and space. If he is to fill his proper role in life, which
is to collaborate faithfully in God's work of creation, he must
begin by accepting this as the starting point of his vocation.
"And *from that point,* however high or low it may be, the
designated task of our life is to climb towards the light, overcoming on our way towards God a given series of creatures
which are not exactly obstacles but rather footholds on the
ascent, mediators to avail us, food to nourish us. . . ." [30] That
is the road to sanctification: "For what is it for a creature to be
sanctified unless it is to adhere with all his powers to God?
And what is that if not to accomplish, in a world organized
around the Christ, the precise function, humble or eminent,
to which . . . he is designated?" [31]

Many churchmen, Teilhard goes on to say (with Luther),
attach exclusive importance to the practice of pious virtues.
Why should others not devote their lives to showing the possibility of the general sanctification of all fields of human

endeavor, in thought, art, industry, commerce, politics, etc.?[32]
To a friend in business who wrote deploring that his work
interfered with his religious aspirations, Teilhard replied:

How, you ask, can the success of a commercial enterprise bring
with it moral progress? And I answer, "In this way, that since everything holds together in a world which is on its way to unification,
the spiritual success of the universe is bound up with the correct
functioning of every zone of that universe and particularly with
the release of every possible energy in it. . . . Whatever we do,
we can and must do it with the . . . consciousness of working,
individually, to achieve a result which is required, at least indirectly,
by the body of Christ." [33]

"By every work we do, we work, atomically but truly, at con-
structing the Pleroma, that is, bringing to Christ our small
contribution towards his fulfilment." [34] As Saint Paul put it,
"Whatever you do, in word or deed, do everything in the name
of the Lord Jesus Christ" (Col. 3:17). By thus participating
in the creative power of God, says Teilhard, "I become not
only its instrument but its living extension"; and "By virtue of
the Creation, even more by that of the Incarnation, *nothing is
profane* here below, to one who can see. Everything is
sacred." [35]

If this vision of the Christian life has a splendid and almost
heroic quality about it, does it not, on the other hand, dangerously blur the classic distinction, rooted in the Gospels and
in Saint Paul, between the world of the flesh and the world of
the spirit on which so much of Christian ethics and its devotional life has been built? If "everything is sacred," what
criterion of choice have we between higher and lower alterna-
tives for action? And what becomes of the Christian virtue of
detachment from the things of this world, beginning with
Christ's command that we should leave all to follow him? The
answer must be found in Teilhard's more subtle and dynamic

distinction between flesh and spirit, on which any understanding of his ethics must be founded:

According to our initial position in our environment, and as a result of our successive situations in relation to it, Matter is divided, in relation to our effort, into two zones: the one already left behind or attained to and to which we may neither return nor attach ourselves without backsliding: that is the zone of Matter in its materialistic or carnal aspect [the *sarx*, or flesh, of Saint Paul]; the other, which offers a new field of progress to our efforts of research, conquest, and "divinisation," is the zone of Matter in its spiritual aspect. And the demarcation between the two zones is essentially relative and mobile. What is good, sanctifying, spiritual for my brother who is below or beside me on the mountain is perhaps bad, perverting, and materialistic for myself.[36]

In each man's life, then, the microcosm reflects the evolution of the macrocosm. First the physical, starting with the union of two cells, multiplies, complexifies, and coordinates itself until its "inside" emerges as consciousness; then the psychic life nourishes itself, centers itself, and expands its web of relationships with the world. And in the individual, as in the world at large, this process cannot fulfill itself completely unless the Logos which directs it through sub-personal forces becomes incarnate for each individual in the Person of Jesus, for "we form, each one of us, a miniature Universe in which the Incarnation takes place independently." [37] Every man, in order that Jesus may enter the heart of his being, must, by faith, give his *fiat* like Mary. But that is only the beginning of the Christian life. For, "God does not present himself to us as something already made which one need only embrace. Rather he is, for us, an eternal discovery and eternal growth. The more we think that we understand him, the more he reveals himself as other. The more we think we grasp him, the more he retreats and draws us into the depths of his Being." [38]

In general, Teilhard says, Christ leads men to himself through the world, and God is to be found in the performance of our allotted task.[39]

In *Le prêtre,* which Teilhard wrote at the time of his solemn vows in 1918, he states his mission in these terms:

To the full extent of my forces, *because I am a priest,* I wish henceforth to be the foremost in knowing whatever the World loves, pursues, suffers; the first to seek, sympathize, labor; the first to develop myself and to sacrifice myself; to be more broadly human and nobly terrestrial than any servant of this World.[40]

And in *La foi qui opère,* of the same year, he says, "Truly . . . only the audacious attain to the Kingdom of God, already hidden at the heart of the World." One must plunge into the totality of things, test oneself against reality, because "all abstract knowledge is a pale reflection of being, because to know the world [conceptual] knowledge is not enough: one must see it, touch it, live in its presence, and drink existence hot from the fount of Reality." [41]

Teilhard often describes the course of a man's life, after his first decisive encounter with Christ, under the image of Jacob wrestling with the angel. In his story, *La puissance spirituelle de la matière,*[42] the angel, who is Christ incarnate in matter,[43] first seduces and then challenges a man to grapple with him, with the double purpose of building him up, leading him to deeper knowledge and mastery of the world and of himself, and at the same time of breaking down his proud and autonomous self-confidence. The struggle is hard, demanding, and finally, unequal. The man begins to fight in order to conquer, fights on for the sheer joy of the struggle; but the harder he fights the more he senses the overpowering grandeur of the reality he seeks to subdue, "until the fever of combat gives way in his heart to an irresistible passion to submit," [44] and in the end "he comes to adore that which he fought against."[45]

So, for Teilhard, "It is a peculiarly Christian duty to grow, even before men, and to make fruitful use of one's talents . . . ."; to search passionately for "Jesus, hidden in the forces which are raising up the Earth"; to labor in order to release a little more spirit by the superior rearrangement of matter.[46] For the human mind is the only force capable of dominating the world, that is, of understanding it and uniting it in love. And love is the supreme virtue, energy, and motive of the Christian life.[47] "The true charity," says Teilhard, "is not moved by the sterile fear of hurting others, but by the vigorous desire to force, all at once, the doors to life. . . ." The struggle involves violence and suffering. "It can happen that I kill my lovers," says the angel, Christ in matter, to his contender.[48] The task is a painful travail and full of risk.

To create, to organize the energies of nature, is an inner torment which wrenches whoever undertakes it from that life of security and tranquility which is the real stronghold of egoism and attachment. To be a worthy artisan of the World, a man must not only quit once for all his peace and quiet, but he must learn continually to leave behind, for yet better forms, the earlier products of his industry, art, or thought. Stopping to possess and enjoy them would be a sin against action. Over and over again, he must surpass himself, tear himself away from himself.[49]

This, according to Teilhard, is true Christian renunciation, the royal road of the cross. So his dicta, "Plunge into Matter! Develop yourself first of all!"[50] are not Promethean or Faustian ideals by which man strives to dominate nature by his own powers in order to stand as a lonely conqueror over a hostile and subhuman world.[51] Rather, the phase which Teilhard calls "the divinisation of our activities" leads to and shades into the phase of "the divinisation of our passivities." The Christ whom he meets in matter is a fire, a spur, a blade. He goads, grinds, purifies those who seek him.[52] And the painful

sacrifice of whatever has become carnal *for us,* whether in
our own selves or in the world around us, by reason of our
own progress through matter is always the price of further
progress toward Christ. The line between what is carnal and
spiritual in matter rises higher and higher as we ascend, so
that "contemplation and chastity tend quite legitimately to
predominate over busy work" as we near the goal. "That is
the general trend of Matter towards Spirit." As in Baptism
and the Incarnation, "Immersion and Emersion, participation
in things and their sublimation, possession and renunciation
. . . [is] . . . the double movement which saves matter by
responding to its challenge." [53]

"There is a time to grow and a time to diminish. . . . But
we should not seek to escape before the time." [54] Christ sees
to it that devotion to life and work brings its own occasions
for detachment. Suffering, obstacles, weaknesses, advancing
age—all contribute to the work of weaning a man of faith
from all that is carnal, inferior, and self-centered.[55] In *Le
milieu mystique,* Teilhard records this prayer:

So that I may not succumb to the temptation which stalks every
bold activity, so that I may never forget that it is you *alone* whom
I must seek in everything, you will send me, Lord, in your own
good time, privation, disappointment, pain. The object of my desire
will fade, or I will rise above it. . . . In the failure of every convenient peg on which I am tempted to fix my life, I have learned
by personal experience that you are the only foundation upon which
I can establish myself.[56]

This is the chalice of Christ's passion, from which every
Christian drinks throughout his life. "For, like Jacob, I shall
not reach God in Matter until I am vanquished by him." [57]

[Therefore,] the Christian is at once the most attached and the most
detached of all men. More convinced than any "worldling" of the

value and inexhaustible interest hidden in the least of terrestrial achievements, he is likewise as persuaded as any anchorite of the emptiness of any success, individual or universal, apart from God. It is God, and God alone, whom he seeks to find through the reality of his creatures.[58]

Our job, then, is to love to the utmost of our strength, that is, to find and to fulfill ourselves in what is other than ourselves. And it is impossible to love Christ without loving others who are also moving toward Christ, and impossible to love others in the context of a comprehensive communion without being drawn closer to Christ. As we give ourselves in work and love to Christ in his community, our own body wears out and diminishes while "our true and universal body continues to grow." [59]

Union in Christ takes place through innumerable acts of love and sacrifice, and ultimate union requires the final and total sacrifice of our carnal selves in death. Death, for the Christian, is thus the last step in the lifelong process of self-giving and ex-centration, by which he has both enriched the gift of his life and prepared himself to offer it wholly to Christ. All through life, Christ transforms our sufferings, failures, illnesses into factors which aid us in our ascent from carnal egoism toward freedom, spirit, and unity.[60] This is the redeeming and transfiguring power of the cross—to turn seeming evil into the servant of positive good.[61] In the light of the cross, "the creative power of death" now effects the final transformation of the apparent annihilation of self into its supreme consummation by rebirth into the immortal body of the risen Christ. For "death delivers us totally to God." [62]

The fight is done; in complete submission, letting go our last grip on ourselves, entering the night of utter trust in Christ, we let him re-create us, and find at last our true selves in him.[63] Once again, the individual, at his death, reflects the cosmos, which, as Teilhard says, "can be consummated only by passing through a death, a 'night,' an inversion, an ex-centration, and a quasi-depersonalization of its elements . . . that is a rearrangement of its whole being preliminary to its re-creation and integration into the Pleroma." [64]

In this perspective, the cross, too often presented to us as a symbol of gloom and constraint, becomes a beacon light toward which we climb, a promise of our fulfillment through a total metamorphosis which can be effected only by the power of our Savior who died for us and was raised. And death becomes truly the gate to larger life. [65]

Teilhard hesitates to elaborate upon the condition of the Christian between his death and the general resurrection in Christ at his Parousia (if indeed temporal notions can be applied here at all). He does, however, seem to presuppose a Communion of Saints in a Church expectant and some form of purgatory when he says that "a well-defined universe . . . goes on building itself above our heads in the inverse direction of matter which vanishes. The universe is a collector and conservator, not of mechanical energy, as we supposed, but of persons. All around us, one by one, like a continual exhalation, 'souls' break away, carrying upwards their incommunicable load of consciousness." [66] Here Teilhard returns to the spatial metaphor which he usually rejects. He goes on to qualify it by saying that there can only be one possible point of definitive emersion—Omega—at the end of the world. More characteristically, Teilhard keeps to his temporal-eschatological schema, as when he says, "We are like those soldiers who fall in an assault which leads to peace . . . even if we seem to succumb individually, the World, in which we will live again, triumphs through our deaths." [67] But the world in which we live again is the Pleroma of Christ, and the individual is transformed into a member of the supra-individual milieu which preserves that which is essential in our present individuality.[68] He is reborn in Christ.[69] In a footnote to page 285 (223) of *The Future of Man*, Teilhard proposes a dynamic relationship between the apparently conflicting ideas of the immortality of the soul and the general resurrection: "The 'collection' of the spirit which is gradually generated in the course of cosmic history is effected in two phases and by two stages: a) first by the continuous 'evaporation' of individual deaths; and, simultaneously, b) by incorporation into the collective organism (the mystical body) which will reach full maturity only at the end of time through the Parousia." If Christ himself awaits the end for his full manifestation, so must the individual who by ex-centration and death has become wholly Christ's.[70]

GRACE, THE CHURCH, AND THE EUCHARIST

Teilhard describes the Christian life as a combat, as a difficult, painful, yet joyous ascent up the rungs of matter, requiring repeated acts of commitment and renunciation. Certain passages taken out of context might give the impression that it is by heroic exercise of his free will power that a man is able to run the course and to say, "I have fought the good fight, I have finished the race" (II Tim. 4:7). But we must remember that if Teilhard rarely speaks explicitly of the underlying activity of grace, it is because he assumes it everywhere. Christ, as Logos Incarnate in all matter, creates and sustains all life, so that man is, properly speaking, "nothing at all apart from him." [71] The gift of grace is the beginning of all our spiritual growth, intellectual and moral. "His prevenient grace is always ready to excite our first look, our first prayer." The initiative is God's, ours the response. Faith, the ability to see, is the "fundamental gift." [72]

Nor can there be any fundamental opposition between man's freedom and God's grace, for man's freedom is itself

the product of God's creative work in evolution. It is, like
the power of conscious reflection, the result of the emergence
of spirit in the form of individual selves.[73] The more highly
evolved, the more conscious a creature is, the more he is
free. So the way toward greater freedom is the way toward the
future and higher consciousness.

On the other hand, our freedom is still enmeshed in the
natural forces which produced it. Our spirit has not fully
emerged, so we are only partly free, and partly still enslaved
to the psycho-biological currents in ourselves. The first act of
emergent freedom, as Genesis tells us, was to cleave to self
(i.e., to the forces of the past) and to reject the will of God
which is to lead us into higher being in the future. But isolation for man is stagnation. Historically, man has gained in
freedom with his association into larger and more complex
societies, but as long as he is bound by self-love he can only
associate under the constraint of law and force. We have seen
how such a society leads eventually to a depersonalizing,
totalitarian collectivity, to the denial of freedom. Similarly, in
man's inner life, self-love ties him to the biological determinisms of his own past.[74] So by choosing self-love man's incipient freedom stunts its own growth and enters a dead end.[75]

Freedom, as one aspect of our spirit's power to reflect and
to love, grows along with our spirit. And in order to grow,
spirit must be freed from its enslavement to the demands of
its carnal matrix. It must turn from the past to the future,
from self to totality, from flesh to the risen Christ.[76] This is repentance—"to change one's mind," in the language of the
New Testament. But our incipient freedom, enmeshed as it is
in its own matrix, can make no such choice unless God in
Christ reveals himself to us, meets us in the flesh, shows us
the way of the cross, attracts us to himself by love. Man is
free to reject God's grace, but still there is no opposition between freedom and grace; for if man rejects grace, it is be-

cause his freedom is not yet sufficiently free. To reject grace is a failure to exercise freedom, and to remain instead enslaved to the law of one's carnal nature. To accept grace, on the other hand, is for freedom to turn and work hand in hand with him who is working to make man more free, to accept the Lordship of him "whose service is perfect freedom." It is to appropriate personally that turning point in the world's evolution at which the universal Logos became incarnate in the Person of Jesus in order to free the world from its determinisms and legal relationships and raise it to the realm of spontaneous union in love. "For freedom Christ has set us free, stand fast therefore and do not submit again to the yoke of slavery." And, "If you are led by the Spirit, you are not under the law" (Gal. 5:1, 18).

Everything Teilhard says about man's efforts in the Christian life must be read in the light of this conjunction of "grace and free will in the infra-experiential layers of the soul." [77] "From you," he prays, "every initiative, beginning with that of my prayer." [78]

Grace, however, does not reject or annul our natural capacities: it illumines them by giving us a goal and a purpose, reorients them and welds them together in a higher synthesis; but it does not perfect us instantaneously.[79] If grace stopped short at revealing our goal, at giving us an example to follow in Christ Jesus, we might indeed have faith and purpose, but where would we find the strength and the energy to surmount the formidable series of obstacles which still separate us from that goal? We have seen that man's natural capacity to love is limited, and cannot carry him far up the arduous ascent toward Christ. To be sure, God's grace, for Teilhard, works universally,[80] but at different levels. Natural man can be led to a certain degree of effort, knowledge, and love by general grace working from within through his reason, sexual instincts, conscience, and without through society. But if he pursues these goals resolutely, he will find himself pressing against his inherent limits. There he will either stagnate in resignation, or else a growing passion and frustration will force him to seek a road to further unity and development, and a superior source of energy for the task. If he cannot find an issue, he may succumb to despair as he presses in vain against the limits of his own resources. But if he encounters the gospel of Jesus Christ and puts his faith in him, he will be led into the community of the faithful in which grace works on the higher level of conscious freedom and personal love. Incorporated by baptism into the body of Christ, he is no longer alone on his ascent and in his struggle. He is now objectively a part of something greater than himself which has an immortal future. Love is no longer limited to a few friends or to mankind in the abstract, but focused on the only object which is at once universal and personal. Christ, in his Church, however, is not only an object of faith and adoration; he is at the same time the servant who gave himself for us on the cross and who gave to his people a supreme means of grace in the Eucharist, in which every Christian can meet his Lord here and now and can eat and drink at the very fount of that energizing love which carries the spirit of the universe upward against the material current of increasing entropy, out of non-being and into eternal life.

We come last of all to Teilhard's treatment of the Eucharist, for it is there that the individual and the collective meet, where the Logos, agent of creation, Christ Jesus who died in Palestine, and Christ-Omega, the future goal of creation, coincide. The whole of Teilhard's theology and cosmology is collected and focused at this point.

The one great purpose of God's creative activity, we should recall, is to call forth the world's emerging spirit in the form of individual consciousnesses and to unite them in a superior synthesis of love with himself. His omnipresence is expressed

by the network of forces which are building up the body of
Christ, and "in this process, Christ himself is not just a passive point of convergence, but a center from which radiates
the energies that draw the Universe to God through his
people." [81] He is also "the organic image of the Universe
thus deified . . . who by the attraction of his love and the ef-
ficacity of his Eucharist, collects little by little into himself
all the forces of unity diffused throughout creation." [82]

From the beginning, Christ works in and through matter in
order to save and transform it; this is the principle both of
the Incarnation and of the Eucharist. In both cases the Word
becomes flesh and the flesh becomes the sacramental vehicle
of the Word. "The word falling directly upon the bread,"
says Teilhard, "transforms it directly into the individual reality of Christ. But the great sacramental operation is not confined to that local and momentary event. . . . there is only
one Mass and only one Communion. . . . from the first
preparations for the Messiah's coming, right up until the
Parousia, only one great event is unfolding in the World, the
Incarnation, realized in each individual by the Eucharist." [83]
Into the immense host which is the universe, Christ enters
and, incarnate by him, it is transformed into his body of
flesh.[84]

It is in humanity as a whole that matter is transformed
for the first time into spirit, and it is in that "consciously
Christified portion of Humanity," the Church, that individual
spirits are united to their immortal body. Christ's death and
resurrection in the past and the communion of every individual
since then form a series of moments which are all part of
one unique activity. "All communions of all men, present,
past, and future, form one single communion." [85]

The Eucharist, however, is not only a celebration of Christ's
giving himself for us. "To the total offer he makes to us we
can only respond by total acceptance. . . . the Eucharist in-

vades [little by little] our whole life until we become wholly his." [86] What began as our receiving ends as total self-giving. Christ's sacrifice on our behalf calls forth and makes possible our sacrifice of ourselves to him. "In this bread, within which you have hidden the seed of all development, I recognize the principle and the secret of the future. To take it, I know, is to deliver myself to forces which will tear me painfully out of myself to thrust me into danger, travail, continual renovation of my ideas, austere detachment of my affections. . . . Lord, I accept to be possessed by you." [87] In *La messe sur le monde*,[88] Teilhard tells how, when on the Western Front and again on the steppes of Asia, lacking bread, wine, and altar for his daily Eucharist, he offered up on the altar of the earth all the labor and sufferings of the world that day to God: "the harvest of today's work . . . whatever will grow . . . or diminish in the World today, everything which will die also, here, Lord, all that I have been able to gather into myself in order to offer it to you, here is the substance of my sacrifice. . . ." [89]

Thus, the Eucharist is also, in the words of Father Smulders, "the sacrament which consecrates the human community to his mystical body . . . as it offers itself to God by virtue of its unity with the sacrifice of Christ." [90] "That we may dwell in him and he in us"—the double action of communion. For Christ in the Eucharist extends his energy and the unifying power of his love through the Church to humanity as a whole, while in the opposite direction, "Humanity assimilates the material world, the Host assimilates our humanity; the eucharistic transformation overflows and completes the Transubstantiation of the bread on the altar. Step by step, it irresistibly pervades the Universe. . . . The sacramental elements are formed by the World as a whole, and the entire course of creation is the time required to consecrate them." [91] The whole drama of creation, redemption, and salvation by the power of Christ's incarnation, death, and resurrection is thus subsumed under the action of the Eucharist. The whole of time is compressed into the few minutes of its celebration. And each individual, by his participation in it, partakes proleptically of the eschatological unity and transformation by which Christ, at his Parousia, will translate the Church into eternal life as his new creation.

and sacraments, raises and consummates mankind. In Teilhard's works, God the Father remains in the transcendent background, while man knows the Father through the Son, his immanent Word, who will deliver all things to the Father at the end of time (I Cor. 15:24). But in his metaphysical discussion of being in *Comment je vois,* Part II, Teilhard applies to God, who "opposes himself trinitarianly to himself," his postulate that "being is to be united"; so that "God himself exists, strictly speaking, only by uniting himself to himself."

In this he reflects Saint Augustine's teaching on the internal relations of love in the divine life. But he does not go on to define the "persons" or their relationships. As in his Christology, Teilhard does not discuss the Trinity in Greco-scholastic terms.[1] Rather, he proceeds directly to the process of creation, whereby from a "createable void" (Fr., *Néant créable*) God begins to unite the elements of a "pure multiplicity"—in other words to give being to non-being—to the end that "no form of opposition may remain unsatisfied (neither interior nor exterior) for the 'pleromized' being," i.e., at the end of time. "Every imaginable possibility for union (whether active or passive) is finally exhausted. 'Being,' having attained this level, is completely saturated." [2]

This is not Teilhard's characteristic vein, but it does shed light on the metaphysical foundations of his phenomenological approach and its Trinitarian background. For if God, the very source of being, is in himself, and prior to all creatures, complex and dynamic, creative and loving, then our idea of God's perfection need not be one which excludes all change and affective relationships. We thus avoid the difficulties involved in relating the static, impassible, absolute monad of rational idealistic philosophy to our finite world of striving, suffering, and becoming; and we make it possible to include God's wrath, and suffering, and redeeming activity in his perfection. In brief, Teilhard's whole thought is based on the Christian assertion that being itself is a complex personal unity bound together by love; so it follows that the world's destiny is rightly to be seen in the same image, reflecting and partaking of the differentiated social unity of its Creator. "Fuller being is closer union; such is the kernel and conclusion of this book," Teilhard says in the Foreword to *The Phenomenon of Man*.[3] But union is not the extinction of differences.

In his brief reference to the Trinity, however, Teilhard does not discuss the nature and functions of the Holy Spirit, and his thought, as he generally exposes it, appears almost to be Binitarian in practice. It is risky and possibly presumptuous, therefore, to attempt any critique of his conception of the Holy Spirit. On the other hand, if we are to relate his thought to the full Christian tradition, we cannot simply overlook his apparent neglect of the third "person" of the Trinity. We should at least ask ourselves whether Teilhard is a reductionist by his silence, or whether he leaves room in his system for the role which has been traditionally associated with the Holy Spirit.

Our problem is complicated by the fact that of all the major tenets of Christianity, the doctrine of the Holy Spirit is among the least well-defined. "The *Pneuma* blows where it wills" (John 3:8), and no dogmatic formulation has ever been able to tie the Spirit down.[4] It is far beyond our scope here to trace all the ramifications of doctrine, so we must confine ourselves to a few basic remarks in connection with Teilhard's treatment or avoidance of the subject.

In the first place, ever since Saint Paul's controversy with those who claimed special inspiration of the Spirit (I Cor. 12:14) and especially since the Montanist schism, the Church has had difficulty reconciling her corporate and apostolic authority with the claims of charismatics and Pentecostals within and without her structure. A theology which emphasizes the role of the Holy Spirit tends to foster (or to be produced by) individualistic sects and to undermine the corporateness and continuity of the Church, qualities which are essential to Teilhard's system. As a Jesuit, moreover, whose own prophetic gifts brought him dangerously close to open conflict with the discipline of the Society, it is not surprising that he should base his doctrine on the person and work of Christ, eschewing reference to the more private kind of inspiration often associated with the Spirit. In this he follows the example of Saint Paul when he declined to combat the claims of opponents by boasting of his own ecstatic experiences, but insisted that the gifts of the Spirit must be tested by reference to Jesus Christ (II Cor. 12; I Cor. 12:1-11).

Indeed, one of the principal difficulties in formulating a distinct doctrine of the Holy Spirit stems from the fact that none of the New Testament writers make any clear distinction between the activity of the Holy Spirit and the Risen Christ after Pentecost, and the two are often used interchangeably.[5] The Old Testament, moreover, makes no certain distinction between God's Word and God's Spirit "who spoke by the prophets"; so anyone like Teilhard with a strong Logos Christology is bound to find less room for describing God's activity in terms of his Spirit. For all these reasons, Catholic theology ever since Saint Augustine has warned against attempts to separate too strictly the functions of the "persons" of the Trinity. *Opera Trinitatis ad extra sunt indivisa.*

It is perfectly possible, therefore, to describe almost all of our experiences of God's activity in terms of Christ without excluding the validity of a parallel description which gives a greater role to the Holy Spirit. It is not an either/or proposition. "We rightly speak of 'Christ in us' for the work of the Holy Spirit in us is to fill us with that life which was in Jesus and to make us living members of the Body of Christ," say the authors of *Doctrine in the Church of England.*[6]

Thus, the distinctive role of the Holy Spirit is at the beginning of the Christian life, as the descent of the Spirit at his baptism stood at the beginning of Jesus' ministry, as Pentecost stood at the beginning of the Church's life. The role which is inalienably that of the Spirit is as the bearer of the grace which opens our inner eyes to the divinity of Jesus, to interpret the Scriptures, to receive a foretaste of the end. The grace of the Holy Spirit is necessary to the Christian life because without it, "No one can say 'Jesus is Lord' " (I Cor. 12:3).

Now, as we have seen, Teilhard does not dwell upon the question of the beginnings of the Christian life. His apologetic aims to lead unbelievers to a confrontation with Christ, but he knows that, in Kierkegaard's terms, the teacher can only provide the occasion, while only God can give the condition of faith. In the works in which he speaks from faith to faith, on the other hand, Teilhard assumes that the beginning has already been made. The Holy Spirit, moreover, witnesses not to himself but to Christ. He who has received the Spirit is enabled to focus entirely on Christ, just as the healthy eye concentrates on what it sees and not on the gift of sight itself, although both are equally important to perception.

It is, then, precisely because Teilhard does not elaborate on the crucial transition from his phenomenological apologetic to his works on the Christian life that he leaves room for, and indeed requires, the action of the Holy Spirit. Teilhard says as much in a number of passages. Though most of them do not name the Spirit they all express the same conviction. To one of these we have already referred in our discussion of grace, for grace, faith, vision, and the Holy Spirit are inseparable in his thought. "His prevenient grace is always ready to excite our first look and our first prayer. . . . The initiative, the awakening, comes always from Him. . . . *Nemo venit ad me, nisi Pater traxerit eum.*" [7] So Teilhard's most basic and fervent prayer is, *"Domine, fac ut videam."* The fundamental and indispensable gift is that of the vision of faith which frees our eyes from the veil of our merely natural perception; which enables us to see the Christ hidden in matter, and to see all things in the light of their future consummation. Without it our experience is of mere facts; history is a meaningless succession of events. Such vision is the starting point for all Christian understanding. "And for that," Teilhard prays, "send us your Spirit, *'Spiritus principalis,'* whose flaming action can alone effect the beginnings and the achievement of the great Metamorphosis. . . ." [8] Nor is the role of the Spirit confined to the beginning and end of the process. His sustaining presence is indispensable. "No sooner does my faith, by misfortune, falter, than the light goes out, everything becomes obscure, everything decomposes. . . . Lord, make me believe." [9]

In sum, it is God's Holy Spirit which enables man to turn from his enslavement and preoccupation with his psychobiological matrix and to embrace the Christ in faith. He reorients our lives and sustains our vision, but he points not to himself but to God in Christ. So we may safely conclude that even if Teilhard speaks rarely of the Trinity or of the Holy Spirit, the one and the other are theological foundation stones, below the surface, but none the less sustaining his whole edifice.

EVIL, SIN, AND JUDGMENT

While Teilhard was in Rome in 1948, trying, among other things, to secure permission to publish *The Phenomenon of Man,* he added, as an appendix, "Some Remarks on the Place and Part of Evil in a World in Evolution" as "my answer (or, if you like, my excuse) to the frequent reproach of naïve or exaggerated optimism." His brief appendix, however, confined to the general, naturalistic framework of the book, does not pursue the problem very deeply and, in fact, calls explicitly for more precision and depth from the side of theology.[10] So our object in this chapter will be to examine Teil-

hard's more theological writings to see just how much precision and depth they can themselves supply to the troubling
question of the role of evil in God's creation, and also to see
why it is that Teilhard, in his writings, is inclined to minimize
its importance.

Teilhard's early writings, like those of Karl Barth, were
conceived in the cataclysm of the First World War. Yet faith
in man, faith in the world, faith in the future are persistent
themes in Teilhard's work. Indeed, his whole life was caught
up and involved in that staggering series of eruptions of hate,
greed, cruelty, and self-righteous isolationism which over-
whelmed the easy, nineteenth-century liberal faith in the inevitability of progress and in human perfectability. Yet there
are pages of Teilhard's which read suspiciously like survivals
of the Hegelian idealism or the Comptian progressivism of
la belle époque, and it is not surprising that, in a period which
speaks its faith through Barth and its anxieties through the
art and literature of the absurd, some should accuse Teilhard
of naïve optimism and insensitivity to the power of evil. It is
quite true that the role of evil is not given a central place in
his works, but it is far from ignored. Teilhard's own life, as reflected in his writings if they are read *in extenso* and in depth,
is a sufficient witness to this, and the specter of evil "seeps out
through . . . every joint and sinew of the system," as he says
himself.[11] There are reasons, both apologetic and theological,
why he does not stress or elaborate the power of evil.

First of all, Teilhard was engaged in *combating* the general
discouragement of his time, and concurrently he was trying to
heal the split between Church and world. He was addressing
himself simultaneously to the churchman disgusted with the
world and to a world disillusioned with itself and alienated
from a Church which seemed to offer it not so much a hope as
a backstairs by which to escape. Furthermore, he was appealing to the surviving optimists—scientists, humanists, Marxists

—who continued to found their hopes upon the quicksands of material progress and man's natural goodness, by proclaiming Christ to them as the only sure foundation and goal of their faith. Hope, not dread, was the key to his message, and here lies the contrast between Teilhard and a Barth or a Kierkegaard. Where the latter would stress the frontier between nature and grace, sharpening the contrast in terms of paradox, scandal, leap, and risk, Teilhard lowers the barrier, builds bridges, speaks of convergence. Instead of driving men to the edge of a precipice and urging them to leap, Teilhard sets up the cross like a beacon and leads men to it step by step. The technique is different and suited to different historical situations, but the aim is the same: to bring men to encounter Christ and put their faith in him.[12]

Even Saint Paul began by feeding milk to men of the flesh and to babes in Christ (I Cor. 3:1f.). The sugar-coated pill as well as the bitter draught has its place in therapy, but only if it has effective medicine inside. A sweetened placebo can be fatal if it deludes the patient into thinking he is cured when he is not. In other words, no preaching or apology can be more effective than the theology which informs it; so we must turn from the apologetic to the theological basis for Teilhard's treatment of evil.

If the creation of the world is seen as more or less complete with the first appearance of man, then an elaborate explanation and theodicy is required to reconcile the idea of a good and loving Creator with the all too evident existence of catastrophes, disease, and sin in our far from perfect world. The myth of the fall is designed to explain this situation, but it raises almost as many questions as it answers (the original state of Adam, the effect of the fall on nature as a whole, etc.); and it has the added disadvantage of confusing the theologically unsophisticated, in other words, the vast majority of men, who, finding it difficult to distinguish between the mythical and historical categories, tend either to historicize the myth, or to reject the myth as pure fantasy.[13] We have already seen how Teilhard transposes the concept of evil, along with his other categories, from a world of fixed essences into one of evolutionary becoming. In so doing he deprives evil of whatever fixed or concrete form it might ever have acquired. Satan, except in Manichaean heresies and extreme puritanism, has always been a slippery and shadowy figure beside the Christ.

In a world which is still in the process of being created, perfection is not to be expected until its final completion, and evil is a necessary if passing element in temporal existence. In this context, Teilhard deals with evil on three successive levels: as physical evil, as suffering on the level of life, and as wickedness on the level of human freedom.[14] Evil begins on the physical level as chaos, disorganization, plurality, conflict, and corruption, that is, falling from a synthetic to a less organized state.

Matter itself, as we have seen, is not evil; on the contrary, it is good insofar as it is responsive, like iron in a magnetic field, to God's creative, organizing power. It is evil insofar as it resists or falls away from higher states of arrangement. Hence goodness is neither an abstract essence nor a property of certain things, but a movement or tendency toward synthesis, spirit, and God. Evil is a falling backward toward the multiplicity and non-being out of which God is creating the universe. Good or evil, moreover, cannot be imputed to any thing or activity in isolation, since the progress of the whole is the only full criterion. So the destruction of one element may be good if it serves the advancement of the whole, even though it seems bad for the element by itself. It follows that only if the universe converges toward a final goal can goodness be clearly defined, and we know it fully only as incarnate in Christ in whom the end is revealed. Evil, on the contrary, has no real being of its own since it is but a residue or a relapse into non-being, and it can be defined only negatively in relation to good, like blindness to sight, or sickness to health. It also follows that evil was not created and hence God is not its author.

Perfect goodness, then, is a transcendental or an eschatological reality. In historical existence, every temporal good is a stage on the way toward perfect goodness. So in history, everything partakes both positively of good and negatively of evil in proportions which vary with the element's position on the evolutionary axis, with the direction of its movement, and with the contribution or hindrance which it makes to the system as a whole.[15]

In this ontological theodicy in which evil is identified with non-being, Teilhard rejoins the conclusions of Saints Augustine and Thomas.[16] But the metaphysical approach of *Comment je vois,* which concludes, "The famous problem [of evil] no longer exists," is not characteristic of his usual existential and phenomenological method. His statement in *L'esprit nouveau* (1942), that evil ceases *theoretically* to be a scandal when it is transposed into a world in becoming, is perhaps a better way of putting it.[17] In another vein he speaks of the existence of forces of evil in the universe which are more than a mere minus sign,[18] and in most of his works, as we have noted, he is more concerned with how to combat evil than in analyzing it out of existence.

Certainly Teilhard's optimism cannot be said to be that of the benign monk or the sheltered academic. "A deadly defect," he wrote in his Journal, "to be obtuse to evil and absorbed in one's own affairs." [19] On the Western Front, in the civil wars of China, and during the Japanese conquest; in the occupation of his own country by the Nazis, in the long and fatal illness of his favorite sister, in his own exile, isolation, and frustration, Teilhard experienced more than his share of suffering and of perverse, organized cruelty. His reaction to the atomic holocausts at Hiroshima and Nagasaki and to the Nazi concentration camps made him a man of our time, fully aware of the power at the disposal of organized evil—or of organized good.[20]

So in *The Divine Milieu* he approaches the problem of evil from the other end, in terms of the battle against evil.[21] That, says Teilhard, should be the Christian's first response to evil. Optimism, then, for Teilhard, is neither an obvious inference from the world nor is it merely desirable for its own sake. Rather, equated with the hope that is born of faith, optimism is a vital necessity in order to call forth and to sustain the efforts and sacrifices required by the battle to overcome the very evils which are deplored by the pessimist. The sense of mission which shaped Teilhard's writings is primarily salutary rather than diagnostic, reconciling rather than judgmental. He aimed not so much to preserve and purify the good by separating it from the bad, as at the more dynamic task of augmenting good and diminishing evil, at overcoming evil with good; and this has never been accomplished by condemning the world from a high pulpit.[22]

To overcome evil with good entails rolling up our sleeves and entering the fray at whatever risk. It means seeing good wherever it may lie potential, and enlisting it in Christ's service. It even means pressing what appears to be evil into the service of good and thus transforming it into its opposite. And since the good, for Teilhard, is a total and eschatological reality, he sees the principal Christian effort in combating evil, not in relieving its symptoms, not in rescuing individuals out of the battle, nor in the charity which succors the victims only, but in the totality of man's efforts to subdue, harness, and share the forces of nature and society in order to release all that is spiritual in them.[23] He would have us attack evil at its roots in the incomplete arrangement of matter and culture, fighting poverty and starvation, for instance, not with hand-outs and soup kitchens only, but by global projects of irrigation, fertilization, research in agriculture and breeding, improved distribution, etc. He would have us fight disease with the whole apparatus of modern medicine and hygiene which in turn depends on prosperity, education, communications, science, and technology; fight against war in the same way, not with defensive armaments only, but by devoting resources, which we now so shamefully waste on trivial or destructive activities, to a massive and collective assault on poverty, prejudice, injustice, illiteracy. And since nationalism, insofar as it has accomplished its work of regional unification, is a residue of division and particularism characteristic of chaos, it is an evil which must be overcome by setting the brotherhood of man as children of one Father in Christ's Church above all national, racial, or class loyalties. So the Church is not over against culture and technology and civil law, but is rather the body through which Christ raises, unifies, and saves the world. It is by engaging ourselves and our resources in all of these fields that we collaborate with God in our own further creation. And the more power man acquires, both in knowledge and energy, the better he is armed in his fight against evil.

The battle is dangerous and the task is costly, the method groping and wasteful. We might well agree that the struggle is good, and yet still deplore the pain which is suffered by the victims, innocent or not, who fall in the conflict. This brings us to the second phase of man's encounter with evil, the problem of suffering.

We have already seen how, for Teilhard, suffering and finally death itself are transformed in the Christian life into positive, creative forces by the light of Christ's cross. But if some men, by their faith, are able to see that their sufferings and frustrations contribute positively to their own and to the world's spiritual development, there are many more, victims of birth, accidents, illness, or senseless cruelty, who simply get "the impression that they are of no use, or even that they are a burden on the face of the earth." [24] The difficulty posed by these "hard cases," Teilhard says, lies in treating them individually. If seen in their total context they become partners in the mighty assault of humanity as a whole on the as yet unorganized forces of the world in which victory is gained only at the cost of many failures and casualties. "They are not useless and diminished elements. They are rather those who pay the price of universal progress and triumph. They are the ones who have fallen on the field of honor." [25] But, "if we seem to succumb [in defeat] individually, the World, in which we shall live again, triumphs through our deaths." [26] "The immense sum of pain in the world appears as the inevitable obverse—as the pre-condition, or even more exactly, as the price of an immense success." [27]

It is with this sense of solidarity and wholeness that we come to the third and highest role of suffering, namely, its power of preparing the world for union with God.[28] For in the world as a whole, as in the individual, pain and frustration liberate the emergent spirit from its carnal matrix and prepare it for the universal ex-centration required for the world's consummation and de-materialization. In this perspective, those members of the body who suffer most and who are most diminished are the very ones who accomplish the highest and most costly of all human roles. And is this not precisely what is expressed in the vicarious and redeeming suffering of the Servant of Yahweh, by whose stripes we are saved, in the beatitude of the meek, the persecuted, and of those who mourn, and supremely in the life and the cross of Christ? (Matt. 5:3ff.).

"In suffering," Teilhard concludes, "is concealed with extreme intensity the world's power of ascension. . . . And is it not exactly for that reason that creation, in the eyes of the Christian, is consummated in the Passion of Jesus? . . . Jesus crucified is not outcast or defeated. He is, on the contrary, the one who bears the weight and bears always higher towards God the progress of the universal advance." [29]

So far, it may be remarked, we have been dealing with the victims of evil rather than with its perpetrators, with the suffering that results from evil rather than with evil itself. If the Christian faith can teach us to see the positive role of suffering and death, then much of evil's sting has already been alleviated. There remains, however, the problem of sin and the sinner, and it is here that Teilhard, in his writings, is least explicit. He explains this oversight in the *Milieu Divin,* his "Essay on the Inner Life," by saying that he is there concerned with the soul already turned from sin.[30] In *The Phenomenon of Man,* on the other hand, which is addressed to the world at large, he states his aim as that of bringing out the *positive essence* of evolution.[31] Nowhere that I know of does Father Teilhard address himself principally to the hardened sinner or to the power of sin. We have already looked at several reasons for this, but are they adequate? Even such a sympathetic critic as the Dominican Father, Olivier Rabut, says that in Teilhard's picture of the world, "we might suppose that the transition from nature to grace would take place quite smoothly . . . but in fact *nature resists grace;* it dreads the transformation asked of it." We are brought back to the contrast between Teilhard and a Barth or a Kierkegaard.[32] Teilhard, however, is well aware of the necessity for a sense of sin and for repentance. Indeed, we have seen that one of the principal values of suffering is to bring this about. But he believes that the surest way to awaken a sense of sin in man and to provoke his repentance is to face him with the full glory of God in Christ. As Canon Raven says in this connection, worship starts with praise of God, not with self-accusation.[33] The negative is revealed as such by confrontation with the positive. Has not Satan always been said to flee at the sign of the cross?

Others criticize Teilhard for failing to make a sufficient distinction between physical and moral evil. "Man is not only imperfect, he can be wicked," Father Smulders[34] insists. But here again, Teilhard is not so much concerned with the judgment to be made upon obdurate individuals (a question we will treat later), but with the objective effects of evil in history and with their subjective repercussions upon the Christian. In this perspective, it can be argued that it is precisely *because* of man's natural resistance to grace that the perpetrator of evil, as well as his victims, has a role to play in creation. In fact, perpetrator and victim are inseparably involved in the same drama quite apart from any intention of their own. If we are able to see, for instance, the contribution made by the victims of Nazi terror or American lynch mobs to arousing the conscience of mankind; if their sufferings helped to overcome the criminal inertia and self-righteousness of the so-called civilized peoples; if the dead and maimed of Hiroshima have consecrated with their blood the atomic bomb into a sacred trust rather than a weapon of aggrandizement—then we can also see that a Hitler, an Eichmann, and all those who contributed to the bomb's making were also instruments of creative providence. So Moses saw Pharaoh, Isaiah saw the Assyrian. So Judas and Pilate made their ignominious but indispensable contribution to the world's salvation. So the men of Christendom called Attila "the Scourge of God." Perhaps this is part of what is involved in loving one's enemies.

A reading of Teilhard's letters reveals how time and again he looked for and discovered the positive meaning for history and man's spiritual growth in the most diverse acts of seemingly unmitigated evil. For example, each war that afflicts us, Teilhard says, serves both to purge us of pride and complacency and also, in the long run, to tie the nations ever more inextricably together;[35] to liquidate the *status quo* and release the germ of the future; to bring about a renaissance.[36]

There is a close parallel between Teilhard's attitude toward the perpetrator of evil and William Blake's idea of the "consolidation of evil" as a creative task. Blake even finds a place in the New Jerusalem at the end of time for the villains of the historical drama because they have so clearly defined and embodied the evil which is diffused through all mankind that it can the more easily be seen for what it is, detested, and cast out. Teilhard and Blake (like the prophets of old) both express this in the image of the alchemy of creation in whose furnace the slag as well as the silver must separate itself into a distinct body.[37]

It is thus difficult to label anything as an unqualified evil, for that which appears in the present as wholly evil may be seen from an evolutionary and eschatological point of view as a necessary, even if painful, factor in the creative process.[38] This brings us to the heart of Teilhard's attitude toward evil in all its forms, expressed succinctly in the phrase, "Providence converts, for those who believe, Evil into Good." [39]

All too often men have tried to solve the classic problem of evil, namely, how to reconcile the omnipotence and the love of the Creator with the presence of evil in the world, by attenuating one or the other of God's apparently irreconcilable attributes. Teilhard, by affirming absolutely both the omnipotence and the love of God, is assured that evil, in time—and proleptically to faith—is transformed into good by the power of God's love. And just as he was enabled, by the vision of faith, to see Christ in the depths of matter, so, looking evil straight in the face, he prays, "My God, since my human dignity forbids that I close my eyes to it, as a beast or a child might do—so that I may not succumb to the temptation of cursing the Universe and its Creator—show me how to adore it by seeing you hidden in it." [40] Such is the sublime power of faith that it enables one to say, "Everything that happens is adorable." [41]

This brings us back by another road to where we concluded with Teilhard's metaphysical argument that evil has no substantial being in God's creation. "Imperfection, sin, evil, flesh, are at bottom a backsliding, an underside of things, which cease to exist for us when we immerse ourselves in God." [42]

We should, however, pause at this point to insist that the faith which sees everything that happens as ultimately adorable is not, as it would certainly appear if quoted out of context, an ecstatic escape from harsh reality or an insensitivity to evil. On the contrary, it depends for its validity upon the confidence that God will overcome evil through man's compassionate, vigorous, and sacrificial reaction against its every manifestation. And such a highly developed faith, moreover, is not acquired easily or theoretically. It is generally the result of long and patient exercise, in obedience to God's grace, in the effort to see Christ in all things, in the battle against evil, in fidelity to one's vocation through periods of blindness and even despair, in prayer and in discipline. We must *force* ourselves to believe, Teilhard says, "all the harder and the more desperately as Reality appears more threatening and obdurate. Then, little by little, we shall see the universal Horror relax, then smile at us, and finally take us into more than human arms." [43]

The very strength of Teilhard's faith in God's loving omnipotence, however, leads Teilhard into problems when he speaks of the world's salvation and judgment. It leads him to a strong preference for an Origenistic universalism according to which all would ultimately be saved and which would thus dispense with a definitive separation of the unredeemed at the Last Judgment.

We have already followed the line of reasoning based on

the phenomena of evolution, socialization, the building and centering of the noosphere, and Christification, by which Teilhard gives the impression that despite many conflicts and reverses mankind will be united by love into one body ready to receive the "spark of the Parousia," which will incorporate it and immortalize it in Christ. This impression of quasi-inevitable salvation, especially insofar as it appears to be based upon empirical observation and inductive reasoning, has offended many of Teilhard's critics.[44] But we have also shown that Teilhard does not impute any certainty to his extrapolations from history, and that the very principles upon which his extrapolations are based are themselves based as much upon faith and revelation as upon observation and induction.

It is impossible, therefore, to have scientific certainty as to the world's future course or ultimate destination. Nor can the firmest faith in God's sovereignty tell us just how, when, or in what form the world will be saved. With the growing emergence of spirit, moreover, man's freedom becomes an increasingly indeterminate and yet decisive factor in the world's history. This in turn risks introducing a growing hazard, namely, the power of sin, into the world's progress; for as man grows stronger in knowledge and mastery over nature, the temptation of self-reliance and idolatry as well as his destructive power may grow apace.[45] "Born with intelligence, the temptation to revolt must vary and grow along with it," says Teilhard, "which explains why it has never shown itself more acutely or universally than at present." [46]

For these reasons, Teilhard is obliged to envision an alternative hypothesis for the end of history. Already we have seen Teilhard speaking of the slag, the waste product, which is separated from the silver in the alchemical furnace. Usually he speaks of this as if it were the material husk which spirit leaves behind it, but he also allows that certain rebellious elements of spirit itself may choose to remain behind in the exterior darkness.[47] Furthermore, as the end approaches and the earth's tensions mount, mankind as a whole will face an ultimate choice between rebellion and adoration, between self-reliant defiance and self-giving ex-centration in a submission to death in order to be raised in Christ. A final conflict may then break out, and humanity may "split into two zones, each attracted to an opposite pole of adoration," in which case "God's universal love will succeed in consummating only a fraction of the world's spirit." [48]

Although this second hypothesis fits uneasily into Teilhard's whole vision, he admits that revelation obliges him to entertain its possibility and that it is "more in conformity with traditional apocalyptic thinking." [49] In this eventuality, the Last Judgment would effect the ultimate separation of the blessed and the damned, and indeed, Teilhard asserts, Jesus Christ cannot be our supreme goal and pattern without at the same time being our judge.[50]

It might appear, then, as if Teilhard leaves us with a choice of two alternative endings, the one of universal salvation which he prefers on evolutionary grounds, illumined by his faith in God's love and omnipotence, and the other derived from apocalyptic prophecies of a Last Judgment. Are we left to pick our own preference between them, or are they somehow related and compatible? I believe that a careful reading of Teilhard reveals a subtle relationship between them in his thought.

"My God, of all the mysteries in which we must believe," Teilhard cries out, "not one so scandalizes our human viewpoint as that of damnation. . . . falling back into non-existence, that we could understand, but eternal futility and eternal suffering!" But, he goes on, "You have told me, My God, to believe in Hell. Yet you have forbidden me to think, with absolute certainty, of any single man as damned." [51] So Teilhard accepts and believes in hell "as a structural part of the universe," and yet he can still cling to his universalist hope. Yes, the *threat* of hell and damnation is always there waiting, the abyss on either side of our ascending path. Because of it, even the most faithful can never give up the struggle and rest easy in confidence that God's all-powerful love will save him in spite of himself. Even hell has its uses in the divine plan. Still, did not Jesus descend even there? And did he not over- come its powers? Is not God strong enough to convert *all* evil into good?[52]

We must be careful not to read assertions into Teilhard's message that are not there, but we might risk interpreting his thought in this manner: that it is necessary for man to believe in the possibility of his own eternal damnation at the Last Judgment (second hypothesis) in order that God may by his mercy save all (first hypothesis). Therefore, we may not assert that universal salvation is a necessary consequence of the world's evolution. Not necessary, but infallible, is the way Teilhard puts it in *The Phenomenon of Man*.[53] Elsewhere he says that the final success is "not only a probability, but a cer- tainty: because Christ (and in him virtually the world) is al- ready risen. This certitude, however, derived as it is from an act of 'supernatural' faith, is itself supra-phenomenal; which means that in a certain sense, it leaves the believer, at his level, with all the anxieties of the human condition." [54]

This is a key sentence. Ponder it, and the whole of Teilhard's theology is reflected in it, particularly those basic questions about the relationship of the objective to the existential, of faith to human knowledge, of the transcendental to the histori- cal, and of eternity to time—questions which are under such intense examination today.

To sum up this chapter, then, we might say that faith is not knowledge, and that it can only exist where uncertainty and the fear of hell abide. At the same time, we must add, faith in God's power and love assures us that "while we were yet enemies we were reconciled by the death of his Son:" that, "He who began a good work in you will bring it to completion at the day of Jesus Christ:" when "He delivers the kingdom to God the Father after destroying every rule and every authority and power . . . that God may be everything to every one" (Rom. 5:10; Phil. 1:6; I Cor. 15:24, 28).[55]

CHAPTER 5

Christianity and Society Today

TEILHARD DE CHARDIN, as we noted in the Introduction, was born into a society radically divided by the secession from established Christendom of a growing, secularized faction. That schism, which first appeared during the "Age of Enlightenment" and cracked open in the French Revolution, was threatening to become an unbridgeable chasm between two camps, as science, philosophy, and politics increasingly detached themselves from their Christian matrix and abandoned faith in the living God as their central and unifying principle.

During Teilhard's youth, major battles in this struggle for men's allegiance were still being fought. Nowadays, militant atheism and anticlericalism are no longer such passionate causes, largely because the secular spirit has effectively achieved its "liberation" from the churches and has very nearly succeeded in confining them to what even many churchmen consider to be their "proper sphere." But unlike the many who have acquiesced in this great retreat, making a virtue of circumstance by stressing the opposition and the superiority of the "religious" to the "worldly" life, Teilhard devoted his life to their reconciliation.

Teilhard was by no means the first, nor was he alone, in deploring the schizophrenia of a disintegrating Christendom; and to understand fully his work requires some acquaintance with the causes and history of this movement toward secular autonomy, and with the various ineffectual attempts to bridge or to heal the split. To supply this background in detail is, however, beyond the scope of this introduction. Here it must suffice simply to note that development in broadest outline, despite the danger of oversimplification, and to refer the interested reader to the Author's Notes and Bibliography for suggestions that will be helpful in studying this background in detail.[1] We should also advise the reader that each side of the split ascribed various causes for the situation and tended to place the onus of blame on the other.

THE CHURCH AND SECULARISM

From Voltaire to Nietzsche, from Hume to Marx, Freud, and Bertrand Russell, leading intellectuals, scientists, and political theorists have proclaimed mankind's liberation from tutelage to the churches—and to the God of Christian theology as they understood it—as requisite to human progress. They blamed the churches for invoking God's sanction in defense of established but obsolete values, privileges, and social structures from the divine right of kings to the absolute sanctity of private property and for engaging in rear-guard actions in God's name against democracy, scientific theories, social legislation, and freedom of speech; so it is not surprising that growing numbers of those whose interest lay in changing the world rather than in defending traditional systems deserted the Church and even asserted that God is dead.

On the other side, church authorities condemned the secular spirit as arrogant, materialistic, sinful, and rebellious; nor did they ever lack evidence of callous injustice, bitter conflict, and inordinate suffering to confirm their denunciations.

But looking back more dispassionately from today's perspective, we might fairly say that blame, if it must be assigned, lay on both sides of the rift and that mutual recriminations have served mainly to drive the opposing parties to further extremes. Surely, if there is to be any prospect of real reconciliation, contrite self-examination and mutual forgiveness is necessary on both sides. Indeed, it can even be said that the whole secular movement has also had its beneficial aspects: purging the churches of pride, unholy alliances, and identification with antiquated metaphysical and social structures on the one hand, and, on the other, liberating men from medieval shackles both intellectual and political and better equipping them, if they will, to carry on God's work in the world. So, as a result of these centuries of revolutionary changes, the chastened churches are coming to see that no immutable form of social structure, no given metaphysical system, are necessary and permanent parts or indispensable vehicles for the Christian faith, but rather features of successive stages in man's total development.

But even if such a catharsis has had certain salutary effects on the churches, the separation of man's life into a religious and a secular sphere cannot be complacently condoned. The Church cannot be true to her incarnate Lord, to her biblical faith, or to her God-given mission by accepting a merely complementary role as one institution beside others, carving out a detached "spiritual" sphere for herself and leaving the world essentially secularized and Godless. Salvation is to make whole and healthy: to heal and to integrate the whole life of men in society; this, and no less, is God's promise in Christ and the mission of Christ in his Church.

The division over the relation of the Church to the world, moreover, exists not only between the Christians and the unbelievers, but between sincere churchmen themselves. Some would continue to battle for a reassertion of churchly authority over all intellectual and political life. Others glorify the Church's liberation from the "corrupting" affairs of the material world and seek God only in the transcendent realms beyond time and space. Still others have reduced their religion to the ethical precepts of a merely human Jesus and to the fellowship of immediate personal relations. For others, religion is a kind of private, individual justification with little relationship to world history and social conditions. Many have sought a compromise between a scientific and a religious world-view by postulating some kind of impersonal deity behind phenomenal reality.

But none of these attempts, whether by the Deists, the Kantians, the Liberal theologians, or the more recent Existentialists, have succeeded both in embodying the full riches and depth of the Christian Gospel and, at the same time, in bridging the gap between man's religious and secular aspirations.

G. W. F. Hegel (1770–1831), a highly controversial figure, was perhaps the first widely influential modern philosopher to propose a way toward overcoming this persistent dualism. His system was no doubt overambitious, overabstract, and it relies too heavily on man's rationality. Certainly he had not the resources of recent scientific and historical knowledge to save him from serious errors. But Hegel, nonetheless, revolutionized metaphysical thinking with his dialectic method, freeing philosophy from its fixed categories and absolute, static ideals. He gave back to historians and to theologians their all but lost Judaeo-Christian dynamic view of history and eschatology as a purposeful unfolding of the divine plan leading to an ultimate fulfillment under God's providence. Hegel re-established time as a critical dimension of man's thinking and history as the theater of God's activity.[2]

The line from Hegel to Teilhard is too tortuous for us to follow here. Hegelian philosophy, separated from its Christian matrix, became an idealist ideology rejected by orthodox theologians both Catholic and Protestant. Indeed, the reaction against Rational Idealism only served to accentuate the rift between Church and world which the scientific and industrial revolution, rising nationalism, and the great wars and depressions continued to widen. Yet through the impetus given to historical studies and especially to an historical approach to the Bible and its theology, through the debates over natural history and over Darwin's theory, certain basic features of Hegel's approach remain. The ultimate unity of all experience, the dialectical path of ascending synthesis toward that unity, the actualization of the Spirit in and through history, the teleological nature of God's providence, the collective aspect of salvation, and a method which combines empirical investigation and rational ordering with historical perspective and synthetic intuition—these were Hegel's legacies to the future and they reappear in Teilhard as in much of modern thought.

Karl Marx, on the other hand, adopted Hegel's dialectic of progress but inverted his priority of the spirit, seeing, instead, all of man's ideals and social values as rising dialectically out of the successive stages of economic development. This dialectical materialism became the metaphysical basis for communism, which succeeded in cleaving a scission through Christendom even more radical than that of the Reformation. Yet despite its utter inversion of values, Teilhard, as we shall see, recognized its deformed kinship—out of Christianity through Hegel—to his own faith in historical progress. As Karl Löwith points out, "The flame of eschatology was kept alive in the nineteenth century not by liberal theologians but by 'atheists' like Proudhon, Marx, and Nietzsche." [3] And it is by means of this link that Teilhard explores the hope of an eventual reconciliation.[4] Who knows whether Marxism may succeed where Christian nations have failed in bringing Asia into the stream of Western culture, and thus prepare the way for a universally re-established Christendom?

But we are getting ahead of ourselves, for outside of its Marxist perversion, idealist optimism was on the wane in the discouraging period between the great wars when Teilhard was beginning to formulate his message.[5] Existentialism and the Barthian theology of crisis were on the rise, while Rome moved with slow caution in the social field and reaffirmed her basis in Thomism. Existentialist theology tended to concentrate on the Gospel's power to transform the individual's subjective life, to save him from the threats of meaninglessness and alienation, and to speak of history as personal rather than universal. The Barthians tended to stress (rather than to reconcile) the opposition between the life of faith and the pursuits of the world. They addressed themselves most effectively to those who were gripped by existential anxieties and by a mistrust of man's capacity for furthering God's kingdom on earth; they had less appeal for those who pressed on hopefully (even if blindly) with their worldly aspirations, more or less content with secular goals. Yet it is these latter who, by and large, are in the saddle of the world's affairs and through whom God shapes the world of the future.

Teilhard, on the other hand, saw that the Church cannot perform her full mission to the world by aiming her message primarily to the hesitant, the introspective, the anxious, or even the pious of the earth. Somehow, if the Gospel of Christ is to guide man's most creative and adventurous endeavors, his apostles must reach those who are committed and responsible for our society's economic, political, scientific, and cultural development. And it was with these same facts forceably thrust upon him that another valiant Christian, Dietrich Bonhoeffer, asked his now famous questions: How would it be possible to "speak in secular fashion of God?" "How can Christ become Lord of those with no religion?" [6]

To find answers to these questions is one of the major challenges which God is making to the Church of our time, and many are struggling to respond to it. But most recent attempts to translate the Gospel into secular terms have fallen into the

old trap of reducing Christian theology to the limits and categories of the particular secular group to which each apology
is addressed. For the *basic* obstacle, as Bonhoeffer himself
pointed out, lies in the very act itself of "thinking in terms
of two spheres." The task before us, then, is not so much to
translate the language of one sphere into that of another—
though this may be a preliminary apologetic device—as it is
to educate the inhabitants of *both* spheres toward a more
comprehensive vision showing the limitations of either one
taken by itself, and to subsume them both into one overarch-
ing, God-centered synthesis. And this is the task to which
Teilhard knew himself to be called.[7]

Only if man's secular work and aspirations are included
within his religion can they be effectively inspired, guided,
judged, and sanctified by Christ's action through his Church.
And this means that the Church must cease to battle in-
transigently against the rising tide of secularization, for to reject it outright is to belie the Church's own faith in God's
sovereignty. As the prophets of Israel warned, we must not
seek refuge in the temple against what God is manifestly doing
in history however contrary it may seem to our habitual values
and cherished schemes.

Like Bonhoeffer, Teilhard sees the rise and spread of
secular culture as a phase in man's coming of age, as his liberation from the laws governing his infancy, and as the growth
of his power to shape nature and society, taking on responsibility for the future. This "liberation" has been won, to be
sure, at the price of an adolescent revolt. Yet surely God
wills men to mature into free, capable, and responsible co-
workers in his creation, and the story of the Prodigal shows
that in some cases a separation and return may prove to be
the way to such a relationship.

By confronting us in history with changes which threaten
our acquired positions and fixed values, Teilhard says, God

spurs us to abandon all our tentative forms of industry, art, and thought. He expels us from the towers of false security which are the real strongholds of egoism, idolatry, and sin. By shaking the foundations of every human institution, to use Tillich's phrase, God liberates us, even against our will, from prisons of our own construction and challenges us to get on with the efforts and sacrifices demanded by his creative plan for our fulfillment, both individual and collective.[8]

"The proper function of Christianity in the World . . . comes down, in my opinion, to this: to quicken [*suranimer*] human enterprise: First by opening up for it an unlimited perspective beyond the closed circle of present-day cosmology: Secondly, by revealing this outcome in a superior Personal Center, not theoretical only, but already partially perceptible in the realm of fact (Revelation, Incarnation). From this double point of view, Christianity appears to me as the supreme motive power of human progress, as the crowning glory of Hominization" (i.e., mankind's ascension toward a unified, complex-centered civilization).[9]

Teilhard, like Bonhoeffer, asked himself why then the Church in practice seems impotent to win and to hold the mass of men. Because, he answers, "Christianity at present, in so far as it fails to include (as it ought) all that is human on earth, loses the cutting edge of its vitality and the voice of its appeal." Without an element of faith in humanity and a common hope, "no religion could appear to man as anything but pale, cold, and inadmissible." "Any religion which is judged to be inferior to our human ideals is a lost religion, however great the marvels with which it clothes itself." [10]

The Church, therefore, instead of holding men to past patterns, instead of fighting change and, worse yet, fanning men's secular hesitations and anxieties in order to keep them in the fold, should be with them in their historic struggles, helping them to respond creatively to change by discovering God's purpose in it, bolstering their faith in the future which God is offering to them, quelling their fears by confidence in God's sovereign love, weaning them from entrenched and beleaguered positions—ever proclaiming Christ, the pioneer of our future, going before us on the way of the cross to victory and eternal life.

But just how, more specifically, should the Church speak of God in a secular way to the Gentiles of our day? Teilhard, cut off as he was during so much of his life from his fellow churchmen and thrown almost wholly on the company of agnostic scientists, humanists, and plain unbelievers, had unmatched resources and occasions to develop the art, and he did so to the point of arousing grave suspicions in his less adventurous brethren. Prevented by censorship from publishing overtly theological work, Teilhard, in hundreds of articles, essays, and lectures, addressed the secular world in its own language and tackled, always from a Christian point of view, a wide variety of concrete and pressing issues from politics, war, and the uses of science to automation, cybernetics, and eugenics.[11] We cannot summarize them all, but as a clear example of how the Christian can address the secular world in its own terms and for its own salvation by raising its sights to that which comprehends it without contradicting its essential thrust, let us examine through Teilhard's eyes what he considers to be the major challenge to contemporary man, one which very nearly includes all the others.

TEILHARD'S RESPONSE TO SECULARISM

The forces which are pressing mankind toward ever greater degrees of socialization or collectivization are irresistible, says Teilhard.[12] A combination of factors already mentioned—the growth of population, the increased specialization and interdependence of men and nations, the more terrible consequences of war, our common battle against suffering and our common search for material welfare, the "shrinking" of our planet before the speed of transport and communication, and mass production—all tend to knit us together in a single web.

"Whether we like it or not, humanity is collectivizing itself; it is being welded into a single whole by planetary forces, both physical and spiritual. From whence the modern conflict in the heart of every man between the element, ever more conscious of his individual worth, and the social bands, ever more demanding." [13]

It is only natural, Teilhard points out, for us to resist, even to fear, the prospect of losing something of our precious independence.[14] But whatever our reaction, we are obliged to respond one way or another to the mounting tide of collective life. And our response is crucial. Not only our present activity and state of mind depend upon it, but man's historical future.

Teilhard wastes little time on the case of those who actively oppose the overwhelming forces of social compression. The whole cosmic ascent from dispersed plurality toward centered unity lies behind our present encounter. The same process which produced man and raised him above every other creature is now urging him beyond individualism to a new stage of ultra-individual evolution.[15] Mankind has now all but completed the divergent stage of his history; he has covered the earth and entered upon the convergent phase of complex unification.

Its first results are not all encouraging: "the ugliness, the vulgarities, the restraints which have undeniably sprung from the industrial revolution . . . even worse, the terrible and growing menace . . . of totalitarianism . . . and worst of all, in a sense, the troubling example of . . . termites, ants, and bees" [16] are enough to make men hesitate or even fight, however desperately, against the inexorable advance of collective life. But it cannot be stemmed, at least not short of massive exterminations, the cessation of modern medicine and mass production, and the total suppression of love. For the partisans of reaction there is no future, no hope, no sense to current history. And yet a significant fraction of mankind, and that in the most Christianized part of the world,[17] stubbornly resists the irresistible while taking its incalculable enrichment of their lives for granted. Uttering a steady stream of complaints against organization, automation, the growth of centralized power and regulation, government planning, heavier taxation, and all the paraphernalia of socialization, men yet continue to flock to the cities, scramble for the products of mass production and entertainment, and look to governments to provide for more and more of their needs. "How, indeed, before this current whose dimensions are not only world-wide but cosmic, can we even think of escaping?" [18]

Merely to resign oneself grudgingly to the inevitable encroachments of socialization, however, is not enough. In fact, such a negative response to deterministic forces leads directly to the very ant hill we most fear. "But man is not an insect. Must we inevitably go under before the inexorable organic determinisms? Impossible! . . . Because man is able to think and plan his activity, he does not submit passively to such laws like an animal; he assimilates and transforms them; he gives them an intelligible moral value." [19] Everything depends, not on the deterministic forces alone, but upon *how man responds to them*.

The fact that we allow the whole process to take place piecemeal and by necessity against our resistance, our wishes, our plans, and even against our "religious" aspirations—this is the real cause of the dislocations, blights, injustices, and social diseases, the superfluous regulations and constraints, which in their turn cause men to stiffen still further their resistance to the march of collective progress.

The contribution that Teilhard and his allies would make to man's secular dilemma is not so much a detailed program —for this must be the cooperative task of experts in many fields; it must be arrived at freely through many experiments and gropings which leave the individual the maximum scope for originality[20]—but a profound change of heart and perspective, an inner change which would automatically change everything around it. This is because all the major problems we face and debate "have two faces and hence two possible responses, depending on whether one considers the human race either as culminating in the individual, or, quite the contrary, as pressing on collectively towards superior states of complexity and consciousness." [21] "It is true that the mass suffocates and neutralizes the elements it engulfs. But why look to an aggregate, a mere heap, as a model of collectivity? Nature offers us numberless examples of associations built up and governed organically by the very opposite principle. In such entities (the only true and natural unities) the association of elements does not annul their differences. On the contrary, *it exalts them*. In every domain of experience *genuine union* (i.e., synthesis) does not confuse; *it differentiates*." That is the essential idea to grasp before deciding for the "Great Option." [22]

"Biologically, as we now see, the human element is not self-sufficient. In other words, it is not in isolation, as one might be tempted to think, but in associating oneself *appropriately* with all others that the individual can hope to fulfill himself . . . Collectivization and individualization (not in autonomy but in personality) are not, therefore, two contradictory movements. The real difficulty lies in shaping events in such a way that the totalization of man comes about, not by mechanical external pressures but by the inner force of harmony and sympathy." [23]

The complementary character of liberty and law, individual

freedom and social obligation, has become a commonplace of political philosophy; but what political philosophy cannot do is to produce the profound change of heart which alone can lead each individual to give himself joyfully and entirely to the collective enterprise. Nor can we expect philosophy or even common sense to generate the inner forces of mutual love, common hope, and willingness to sacrifice—on which our progress depends.

Teilhard says, "Union, far from diminishing men, stimulates them, enriches them, and elevates them beyond themselves. The true union, the union of heart and spirit, does not subjugate, does not neutralize the associates. It *super-personalizes them*." [24] He has carried us almost imperceptibly across a frontier, or rather, has raised us over a threshold. He starts to address the secular humanist in his own terms with physical and biological analogies, only to reach and demonstrate their limits. The biological model is superior to the mechanical but it cannot suffice for the future of society. Men are not destined, if they respond creatively, to become mere cells in a Leviathan. When we look to the future, we must shift from analogies from below to analogies from above, from science and philosophy to religion. "What at this point impedes our advance or even halts the march of the spirit is evidently the seeming impossibility for us to imagine something emerging from nature as we know it that is more organically complex and psychically centered than the human type." [25]

Faith in progress must look not to some "pitiful millenarian ideal," some "golden age." "Before such a 'bourgeois' ideal our hearts quite rightly fail us." It is not so much a question of *well-being* as of *more-being*.[26] "A common interest, however passionate, brings men together only indirectly and around an impersonal, depersonalizing center. It is neither a *tête-à-tête* nor a *corps-à-corps* but a heart to heart contact that we need. To meet these conditions, the more I examine the fundamental question of the World's future, the more I become convinced that the generative principle of its unification is finally to be sought neither in the contemplation of a common truth alone, nor in the desire for a common object, but in the common attraction exerted by one and the same *Person*." [27]

"Only a union effected by love . . . because it gathers men, not superficially and tangentially but center to center, has physically speaking the power not only to differentiate, but to personalize the elements which it organizes . . . by internal mutual affinity. But these very forms of attraction, on which our unification is postulated, do they not basically depend upon the radiation of some ultimate center (at once transcendent and immanent) of psychic convergence?" [28]

We need not repeat all that was said in Chapters 2 and 3 about the indispensable role of Christ and his Church in the unification and transformation of humanity. We are concerned here only with its relevance to Teilhard's attempt to overcome the split between Church and world, between the "religious" and "secular" viewpoint. But Teilhard's full view of history as "Christogenesis," and of the Church as the spearhead of man's future evolution, must be kept firmly in mind if we are to follow it.

The fact is that Teilhard does not see the basic split in humanity in the conventional categories of Christian versus secular, or of totalitarian versus democratic. These are false dichotomies. The real division is between the "fixists" and those who believe in progress, and then between the "pluralists" who see only a self-limiting, divergent evolution and the "monists" who see everything converging toward some higher form of consciousness.[29] These much deeper cleavages cut right across institutional lines, dividing churchmen between the merely "religious" (or "spirituals," as Teilhard calls them after Saint Paul)[30] and those with faith in a world-process culminating in Christ-Omega; and dividing likewise the secular camp into conservative individualists on the one hand and progressive, humanistic socializers on the other.

The first of each of these two groups, within and without the Church, form natural allies against the Christian and non-Christian advocates of collective progress. And it is toward the synthesis of these latter, allied but mutually misunderstood groups that Teilhard is pressing. "Christian or non-Christian, those men who are animated by this particular conviction *form one homogeneous category*. Even though found at the two extreme wings of advancing humanity, they can march hand in hand without equivocation because their attitudes, far from excluding each other . . . only need to complete one another." A "common front" of these two parties could form "the solid nucleus around which the unanimity of tomorrow is destined to grow."

Faith in "the Above and the Future, two religious forces . . . which fail and perish if kept apart—two forces, therefore, . . . which await only one thing; not that we choose between them, but that we find the means of combining them one with the other." "Here an expanding Center in search of a sphere: there a sphere coming to self-understanding and in need of a center." [31]

Teilhard represents this resolution in a simple diagram in which the "spiritual's" faith in a transcendent God is the vertical axis and the humanist's faith in man's ability to build a better world in the future is a horizontal line. These two tendencies, though divergent, are not opposed. Either is incomplete, and the direction Teilhard proposes to us is the resultant of the two: a diagonal vector rising and advancing at one and the same time. "Followed to the end these two paths are bound to meet. For, by its very nature, whatever is of faith rises, and whatever rises inevitably converges." [32]

For one who has had his eyes opened to such a faith, to the synthesis of "the Above and the Future," the whole aspect of the contemporary movement toward socialization changes. Without blinding him to its cost and inconveniences, it takes on an immense and personal value which makes the cost seem light. From a victim of irresistible and incomprehensible forces, from a mere cog in the machine, this faith transforms him into an enthusiastic collaborator in the cosmic process.

Irresistible: for the man of faith that means the will of God—nothing else is irresistible—and the will of God is good. The man of faith responds in gratitude for the very forces which seem to be crushing us together from every side. It is they which force us to reflect and respond creatively, to strain every resource of technique and invention to meet their challenge; it is they which oblige us to try every possible form of organization in order to find the best, to think and to plan in ever greater mutual solidarity, to expand our love in ever wider circles. In our response to them we can discover the first limbs of that superior unity which alone can "raise us through more centered complexity to a higher degree of consciousness and personality," and, we might add, to a greater degree of freedom, since the more the whole is complex and centered, the more freedom it enjoys.[33]

So, says Teilhard, "Instead of trying to negate or to minimize, against all evidence, the reality of this great phenomenon, let us accept it openly, look it in the face, and see if we cannot build upon its indestructible foundation an optimistic edifice of joy and liberation." [34]

Only the vision afforded us by such a faith in the above and beyond will enable us to respond creatively to the deterministic forces which press on us from below and behind. And our response will make the difference as to whether we are to be passively or protestingly regimented, mechanized, dehumanized, or even exterminated, or whether we seize the occasion God is offering us to collaborate in building up the body of Christ in which alone we have our eternal life.

In this faith and confidence, then, "there is nothing else to do than to plunge resolutely, head on—even if something of ourselves must perish—into the crucible of socialization. Even if something must perish? But where is it not written that he who loses his life will save it?" [35]

What is the place of worship and prayer in a "worldly Christianity"? After all we have said here and earlier[36] about the necessity of an actual, concrete, personal, loving and lovable center of convergence; of God's grace; of membership in Christ's body on earth; of proleptic participation in the eschatological community; and of direct communion with Christ in the Eucharist, the answer should be clear to all.

Of all forms of faith, religious and secular, Teilhard proclaims, "Christianity emerges decisively in the lead with its extraordinary power to immortalize and to personalize in the Christ, so as to render lovable the whole evolution of time and space." [37]

We should recall here Teilhard's dictum, "The work of the world does not consist in giving birth to some reality within itself, but in fulfilling itself by union with a pre-existent Being." [38]

Nothing less than a passionate faith and adoration which devotes a man's whole being to the crucified and risen Christ can fill him with that unflagging confidence in an immortal consummation of the world's travail which is absolutely indispensable to man's ultimate victory by the grace of God over the inner obstacle of egocentric sin and the outer task of subduing the material universe and preparing it for its transformation at Christ's Parousia into God's eternal kingdom of love.

CHAPTER 6

Teilhard's Methodology

"ALL ABSTRACT KNOWLEDGE is a pale reflection of being . . .
one must see, touch, live in the presence of Reality, drink
existence hot from its fount." Teilhard warns us of "the empty
fragility of the most attractive theories compared to the sub-
stantiality of the slightest fact taken in its concrete and total
reality."[1] He asks us to read *The Phenomenon of Man,* "not
as a work on metaphysics, still less as a sort of theological
essay, but purely and simply as a scientific treatise." [2] In a
similar essay he says, "I affirm and I maintain that throughout
the pages which follow I never leave for an instant the realm
of scientific observation." [3]

Despite Teilhard's contentions, however, anyone who has
even a high school familiarity with science (one might venture
to say *especially* those who have had only an elementary course
in science) could object that his arguments bear no resem-
blance to scientific texts and indeed go far beyond the disciplines and limits of scientific method. Teilhard's talk of an
imperceptible psychic "within" of matter, of "spiritual energy," of teleologically directed evolution is already scientifically suspect, not even to speak of such notions as the
"noosphere," "super-consciousness," the "hyper-personal,"
and, above all, Christ-Omega and immortality of the emergent
spirit.

"Mysticism remains the great science," Teilhard wrote to

his fellow paleontologist-priest, Abbé Breuil, in 1923.[4] Perhaps, some may suspect, Teilhard's "science" is in fact a mere vehicle for Christian apologetic or indoctrination, to demonstrate that "the most traditional Christianity . . . is susceptible of translation into terms which embrace the best aspirations of our times"—to paraphrase his Preface to *The Divine Milieu.*

Teilhard was well aware of such suspicions and genuine perplexity as to his methods; he encountered them and wrestled with them all his life long. "Among those who have attempted to read this book to the end," he says of *The Phenomenon of Man,* "many will close it, dissatisfied and thoughtful, wondering whether I have been leading them through facts, through metaphysics, or through dreams." [5] This chapter is addressed especially to those wondering and dissatisfied readers whose scientific training (and whose way of thinking has not been at least partly shaped by the methods of science?) forbids them to follow Teilhard's arguments to the end.

We have said a good deal about Teilhard's method in the course of our study in connection with various matters as they arose. But at the expense of some repetition, let us reverse the procedure and gather some of Teilhard's scattered remarks on method into a systematic examination of the relation of his approach to that of science. Indeed, speaking of *The Phenomenon of Man,* Elizabeth Sewell, in her highly perceptive *The Human Metaphor,* predicts that the most lasting value of his book may be methodological.[6]

SCIENCE, PHILOSOPHY, AND FAITH

Ever since the curtain of the Enlightenment descended upon the European mind, prophets like Hegel and William Blake have protested against the narrow vision imposed on those who don glasses prescribed by Locke, Hume, Laplace and

Co., and against the split vision induced by the object-subject, perception-intuition, and matter-mind dualism of Descartes and Kant. But prophetic voices were eclipsed by the success of positivistic science. A narrow vision is often an advantage in accomplishing a given task, and the very elimination of human, moral, and theistic considerations from their fields freed scientists to experiment and to analyze matter in a way impossible under previous presuppositions. They had to shake the incubus of a God who interfered arbitrarily in the material workings of his creation off their backs and to clear the scales of medieval superstitions from their eyes. Such indeed was the success of physics and its closely related pursuits that its strictly delimited methods were extended indiscriminately even to such fields as history and psychology. A number of modern historians have recorded this trend.[7] The present generation, however, is witnessing a renaissance of the broadening, deepening, and far-searching spirit of enquiry after more than a century devoted largely to more prosaic investigations which have furnished the current renaissance with a store of facts, principles, and a respect for experimental and historical data far superior to that of their predecessors.

Here again, we must rely on the work of men who have specialized in tracing this revolution in the scientific outlook and refer to them for the concrete data and illustrative examples on which the necessarily bald assertions which follow are carefully founded.[8] A reading of Polanyi or Kuhn should give a sufficient taste of the current re-examination of scientific knowledge, or rather its epistemology, to enable one to place Teilhard in the mainstream of scientific thought and to understand how he could say, toward the end of his life, that he had "invented" nothing, but was simply a sensitive "resonator" to vibrations which were everywhere in the air and needed only to be amplified and expressed.[9]

We must begin by describing what Kuhn calls "normal

science," namely, "research firmly based upon one or more past scientific achievements," acknowledged by a scientific community, and taught through textbooks which expound a body of accepted theory.[10] Students are taught by these texts and their teachers to envision reality according to the model of the universe, with its categories, laws, symbols, and relationships—the method which is currently favored by the authoritative leaders of the prevailing scientific community, those whom Teilhard calls "the pontiffs of science." [11]

The vast majority of all scientific work is carried out within this framework. Experiments are designed to verify or fill out its predictions; research is directed toward goals which are envisaged and selected on the basis of its assumptions. This is what Kuhn describes as the "priority of paradigms," Polanyi as the primacy of the conceptual framework, and what Teilhard calls "a general condition to which all theories, all hypotheses, all systems must bow and which they must satisfy henceforward if they are to be thinkable and true." [12]

This is the fundamental point on which the following argument depends, namely that, as against the widespread notion that scientific method begins with an unprejudiced, objective, detached openness to nature and observation, quite the contrary: a scientist can make neither head nor tail out of the inexhaustible multiplicity of his perceptions, nor can know where to direct his attention, nor can he ask the kind of questions which lead to specific experiments, nor can he organize the data he receives; he can do none of these essential operations without *from the start* having a more or less ineffable, but none the less determinative framework or related presuppositions about the nature of reality and its workings. All particulars are meaningless (i.e., unrelated) unless they are seen as parts of a mental pattern into which they fit rationally. But the overall pattern is *ipso facto* not derived from the perceptions which it organizes, nor can it ever be fully expressed "for assertions can only be made within a framework [of pre-suppositions] with which we have identified ourselves for the time being. As they are themselves our ultimate framework, they are essentially inarticulate." [13]

As Teilhard says in his Preface, "Every experience, however objective it may seem, inevitably becomes enveloped in a complex of assumptions as soon as the scientist attempts to explain it. But while this aura of subjective interpretation may remain imperceptible where the field of observation is limited, it is bound to become practically dominant as soon as the field of vision extends to the whole." [14] These presuppositions are hidden in our very language, our ideas of space and time, systems of classification, and so on. Nor are these categories innate to the human mind, as Kant would have it. Rather they are acquired by the would-be scientist (and many others besides him) by submitting himself in advance to the authority of the prevalent scientific community and its standards.

Normal science thus pursues its work of fitting more and more pieces into its overall picture of nature as long as there is a broad consensus of basic tacit assumptions among authorities. This normal procedure is what gives the impression that scientific knowledge was acquired by a long accumulation of observed data, the progressive refinement of techniques and instruments, and the extension and verification of theorems by experimental reference to objective reality itself as the final authority.

There is much truth in this view if it is confined to the elaboration of any given scientific theorem, but it explains neither the evolution of man's scientific view of reality nor its relation to reality as such, as any serious study of the history of science and its successive revolutions will show. The trouble is, as Kuhn points out, that textbook science does not proceed historically like other disciplines which present students with successive and rival world-views, but instead tends to bury its own vital history and present only the *fait accompli* and to view the past only as interpreted in the light of its present conceptual framework, thus making the history of science look linear or cumulative.[15]

But as soon as we shift our attention from the specific results of scientific research to the basic premises about reality out of which they grow and to which they refer the whole picture changes. We no longer see linear growth and steady improvement, but instead a succession of dead ends; crises; new intuitive hypotheses, "a series of illuminations," as Teilhard says,[16] coming to noncomforming individuals of imaginative genius and followed by protracted battles between rival schools of thought; a lengthy process of experimental verification, *ex post facto,* of the new set of assumptions; passionate resistance to change on one side and equally passionate attempts to make converts to the new school on the other. For a time there are two sciences. Man is faced with a choice between two virtually exclusive systems, each of which claims better to organize and explain the available data.

One of the most striking of these crises in the evolution of science, and certainly the most easily visualized by the non-specialist, was the Copernican revolution. But there have been many others: the switch from the phlogiston to the oxygen theory of combustion in chemistry for instance, or the switch to Dalton's theory of atomic compounds. Each altered the scientist's basic picture of matter, just as the acceptance of Freud's postulate of the unconscious (after years of fierce resistance) transformed man's image of his own reason and psyche, and Einstein's theory revolutionized the Newtonian framework of time and space within which every observed event takes place. Each of these revolutions in science teaches the same lessons, which we shall sum up as briefly as possible, referring to sources for the evidence and for its interpretation.

(a) There is no gradual, step-by-step transition possible from one basic paradigm of nature to another. Either the earth *or* a point within the sun is the center of our planetary system. There is no middle ground. Copernicus forced men to choose, one way or the other; nor could he produce any compelling empirical evidence. The observed movements of the planets could be explained and predicted as accurately by the Ptolemaic astronomers as by Copernicus, and their geocentric viewpoint certainly corresponded to man's common experience of watching the sun and stars rise and set. A real act of faith was required to see everything differently, and more than a century of heated controversy was required to convert the authoritative community to the Copernican model. Human knowledge grows, Teilhard says, like the evolution of life toward higher forms, by successive "mutations, more or less brusque; and revealing, beyond a simple development of human ideas, an evolution of the 'space' within which all ideas are formed—a process which is evidently far more stimulating and more fundamental." [17]

(b) The origin of a new and revolutionary picture of nature is, therefore, not the outcome of "normal" scientific research pursued within its commonly accepted framework. On the contrary, "normal" science quite rightly tends to ignore, circumvent, or explain away any anomalous observations which do not fit into and support its canons.[18] Only after a prolonged period of crisis, after repeated failures to deal with persistent complications and anomalies, will a rival paradigm of interpretation be seriously considered. "Paradigms," says Kuhn, "are not corrigible by normal science at all." And history shows that the new model is almost invariably proposed by one or more younger men, even by relative amateurs in their field, who are not as deeply committed as most professionals to the prevailing presuppositions.[19]

The heart of Polanyi's work on scientific method lies in his study of heuristics, that is, of the process by which basically new discoveries are made by geniuses of real originality. He stresses the initial role of passionate faith that an as yet unsuspected solution to a problem does somewhere exist and will reveal itself to persistent search. He describes the alternation between periods of concentrated calculation and experiment, and intervals of almost passive contemplation and incubation of ideas—of waiting expectantly for something to present itself to the imagination. He records the experience of "illumination," receptive intuition, and sudden conviction, to which so many discoverers have testified. Furthermore, Polanyi says, "The most daring feats of originality . . . must be performed on the assumption that they originate nothing but merely reveal what is there." [20]

Describing his own experience, Teilhard says, "At that point, I felt rising within me, against all convention and plausibility, a sense of that which ineffably relates all things to each other. The supreme unity communicated itself to me by giving me the capacity to grasp it. I had really acquired a new sense—the sense of a new quality and dimension. Even deeper, a transformation had taken place in my very perception of being. Being itself became from then on, as it were, tangible, poignant." [21] It is out of such experiences of illumination and revelation that all genuine discoveries come.

(c) The experiments, instruments, and observational data used to support a new theory are developed *after* and *because* certain men are converted to faith in its ability to provide a more comprehensive and coherent picture of reality. Only when someone is at least tentatively committed to a new paradigm is it possible for him to ask the right questions, to devise and perform the experiments necessary to verify and extend its objective consequences.[22] Indeed, the decisive factor in the eventual acceptance or rejection of a newly proposed, revolutionary conception of nature is not its immediate success in organizing all available data, but rather its subsequent fertility in guiding its adherents toward wholly new discoveries which were quite unexpected when it was originally proposed and which were inconceivable to its opponents.[23]

A newly proposed theory, in other words, does not present itself with incontrovertible experimental proof, but, stemming from an intuition, it challenges men to make a choice based first of all on its appeal to their sense of its rational coherence —its ability to give an overall structural understanding of the relevant data, then on its ability to suggest and inform further research. "Coherence and fertility, the two criteria of truth," Teilhard says, and challenges his reader: "illusion or truth . . . it is up to you to choose." [24] And in *Comment je vois,* he says that the special characteristic of truth is its power to unfold indefinitely in such a way that all the parts are gradually brought into significant relationship with each other.

Once again, it is not to some impersonal "objective reality" to which the choice is referred, but to man's mind, his ability to recognize a rationally satisfying pattern. "Object and subject marry and mutually transform each other in the act of knowing; and from now on man willy-nilly finds his own image stamped on all he looks at." [25]

(d) We have seen that the path to original and creative "mutations" in scientific thought is not one of logically connected steps nor the way of "normal science." It is a leap across a "logical gap" between the established system and an as yet untested, sketchily delineated, largely ineffable intuition of possible relationships. Such a leap, like that of a spark, requires a build-up of voltage; it requires passion, courage, and faith to motivate it.[26] These personal and emotional factors are not involved in discovery only. Because of the logical gap between competing systems, the authoritative scientific community is split in two. There are now two schools, and their respective partisans cannot convince each other by logical argument—logic being the rules for the manipulation of terms and symbols *within* a commonly accepted framework.[27] Nor can they prove their contentions by reference to experimental data alone, because the same data will be interpreted and evaluated quite differently on either side of the gap. No system satisfactorily explains *all* relevant data. If it did, the real progress of science would cease forthwith. A newly proposed paradigm will explain some of the data less well than its rival. It will invariably raise a host of new puzzles as well as solve old ones. All these considerations will be used by its opponents against its acceptance. And no one who is truly wedded to the axioms of "normal science" can make the leap. On the other hand, the apostles of the new view will seek to make converts by every means, appealing to aesthetic, rational, moral, political, and religious feelings.[28]

Each contender must attack not only the details of the other's system but its most basic assumptions. And so fully are a man's mind, his very perception of reality, and his subconscious mental processes identified with his tacit conceptual framework, that to attack it is not to attack some idea of an objective, impersonal reality but to attack the man himself in his very person. This is why scientific controversy so often involves vicious attacks and counterattacks on the contestant's motives, intelligence, and integrity—so far is the scientific attitude from its often-vaunted objective detachment.[29]

Often a whole generation of established authorities has to die before a promising new theory can fully establish itself. But, says Teilhard in *Le Christique*, nothing is so strong as a truer idea. Once it appears in a single mind, nothing can stop its light from spreading. "From the moment that a few men began to see the world with the eyes of Copernicus, all men began to see in the same way. An initial illumination, intuitively accepted regardless of the risks of error, and then gradually confirmed by experience, became definitively integrated into the hereditary nucleus of man's conscious thought." [30]

THE ETHICS OF SCIENCE

With this much attended to, we shall list several other related principles.

(a) Since perception itself and all interpretation of its data depend upon our overall conceptual framework, we must revise any lingering, naïve notion of "factuality" we may have. Unless we reserve the word "fact" for the raw impulses which reach a passive brain through the nervous system, every perception is in large measure a product of what we believe and every assertion of "fact" is an assertion of personal belief, of commitment, that is, to the whole system of beliefs within which a given phenomenon appears to be what we take it to be. "There is no fact which exists in pure isolation," Teilhard says.[31] Two eighteenth-century chemists and an animist, for example, might point to the same fire; one would say it was releasing its phlogiston, the other that it was consuming oxygen, the third that its demon was angry. We tend to laugh down those who interpret experience in terms of a different paradigm from our own. They appear almost insane. But we should remember that the universe of Copernicus and Newton is almost as strange to modern science as the Ptolemaic was to them, and we have no assurance that our present picture of reality is any more stable or final. On the contrary, history and the plethora of current problems and competing hypotheses in contemporary science should keep us ready for drastic alterations in our most cherished assumptions. Indeed those who reject, out of hand, the "factuality" of whatever is strange and incommensurable with their beliefs will contribute nothing to the expansion of man's conceptual capacities.

(b) Conceptual systems are not innate to the human mind, though the capacity to form or to acquire them must be. They are ordinarily acquired not by reference to nature (else we should all grow up with geocentric perceptions) but by submitting ourselves against all appearances and common sense to the authority of those people, beginning with our parents, in whom we have confidence. As we grow up we absorb by and large the presuppositions of the community to which we commit ourselves. Our very language carries within it our most fundamental assumptions about reality.

Science, then, at any given time, is that body of beliefs which is shared by what Polanyi calls a mutually accrediting community. Thus, a man's beliefs, with rare exceptions, are based on personal commitment to his community, but they are not personal in the sense of individually arrived at by random experience or by his own empirical experiments.

The science of any given community, therefore, depends wholly upon its hierarchy of values and its social organization. If it puts either the production of a certain type of goods or the quest for political power and party aims above its respect for truth, as yet undiscovered; if it fails to respect the integrity of the individual above immediate considerations of the group's welfare; then genuine science will perish from that community. Potential scientists will then become the servants, not of their quest for truth, but of their political and commercial masters. Research will be directed wholly toward expected, practical results. Truth will be defined, not by science, but by the propagandists of the ruling party's ideology. "Facts" will be manufactured, conflicting evidence will be suppressed. Dissenters will be starved, expelled, or "liquidated." Education, textbooks, and "history" will be manipulated for ulterior reasons. The society will insulate itself from rival systems of thought. In short, whether genuine science stands or falls depends upon whether a society places moral values, respect for persons and for truth, above any material advantages or ideological aims.[32]

The progress, even the very survival, of modern science depends, moreover, upon man's success in responding creatively and morally to the pressures of socialization. No single man, no isolated group of professors, can acquire or master more than a tiny portion of scientific knowledge. Science is a collective possession, research a collective task. It depends not upon professional scientists alone but on a world-wide structure of government, industry, education, and communications. And if it is to progress, to draw an ever truer picture of our universe, science cannot exclude moral values from its purview. "In turning reflectively on itself," Teilhard says, "evolution moves into the moral sphere in order to progress." [33] Polanyi puts it thus: "Science can then no longer hope to survive on an island of positive facts, around which the rest of man's intellectual heritage sinks to the status of subjective emotionalism. It must claim that certain emotions are right: and if it can make good such a claim, it will not only save itself but sustain by its example the whole system of cultural life of which it forms part." [34]

Nor can the scientist afford to reserve judgment on moral questions which affect his society. The skeptic's and the agnostic's alleged hesitation to adopt a proposed system of values until convinced by better evidence is a mere pose. A man's every thought, word, and action stem from an underlying hierarchy of values, conscious or unconscious. Life constantly forces him to act one way or another. Not to act is itself a moral act. Not to adopt a given system of values, then, is to positively reject it and to act on some other system instead. There is no neutral position.[35]

Of course many an eminent scientist is vitally interested in the moral life of his community. But for many of them, are not their ethical and religious beliefs quite disconnected from their scientific knowledge? The moral believer and the professional scientist often dwell together for better or for worse in the same skin. What Teilhard offers is a method by which the two domains can be intimately and dynamically linked, so that each informs the other. For in Teilhard's world, love (in its widest and deepest sense) "enters into the scientific realm of cosmic energies and necessary laws." [36]

(c) We have already said a good deal, in the body of this book, about the contrast between analysis and synthesis; it lies near the heart of Teilhard's methodology. Analysis, he says, is a marvelous instrument of science. It gives us a detailed inventory of nature and its workings. It traces the anatomy of things back to their simplest components. It provides us with working laws of cause and effect which enable us to predict and to manipulate natural processes. But at the same time, it turns our attention away from the whole, the more complex, the qualities of consciousness and freedom which reside in a total, undivided organism. It attempts to explain the higher in terms of the lower, the present in terms of the past and its determinisms. "Breaking down synthesis after synthesis [it] allows one soul after another to escape, leaving us confronted with a pile of dismantled machinery and evanescent particles." [37]

This attempt to explain all in terms of the simplest elements is what Polanyi calls the Laplacean fallacy—the ideal goal of positivistic science being to explain all experience ultimately in terms of the position, movement, and energy of every atomic particle in the universe.[38] The whole future of the universe, according to Laplace, could theoretically be calculated from such data. The observer and manipulator of nature, the scientist himself, was completely left out of this impersonal picture of the cosmos—a cosmos from which mind was excluded and hence science impossible.

"We are surprised," Teilhard says, "to see how naïvely naturalists and physicists were able at the early stages to imagine themselves to be standing outside the universal stream they had just discovered. Almost invariably subject and object tend to become separated from each other in the act of knowing." "Physics, absorbed in its analytical work was dominated by the idea of the dissipation of energy and the fragmentation of matter. Recently, however, recalled by biology to take the effects of synthesis into account, physics begins to see that, balancing the phenomena of corpuscular disintegration, the universe, looked at historically, displays a counter movement as general and profound as the first"; namely, the synthetic building up of complex entities culminating in consciousness, man and modern society in the present, and pointing toward the noosphere in the future.[39]

Yet, after a century of dispute, "the quarrel between materialists and the upholders of a spiritual interpretation, between finalists and determinists, still endures. . . . Both these and those fight on different planes and do not meet; each sees only half the problem." [40]

Analysis looks downward and back toward more simple elements and greater subdivision. Synthesis travels the other way, tracing the complexification and unification of things. It looks to the future also, and seeks its unifying principle in a point of convergence and maturity, just as we understand and try to guide the growth of a child by reference to what we know a man to be.

So, since geology, biology, and evolutionary theory introduced the dimension of historical time into the realm of science, linking the increasing complexity and synthesis of matter to the emergence of consciousness, science can no longer afford to ignore man and exclude the fact that evolution produced mind from its image of the material world—that is, science in its broadest sense. For in its departments which deal exclusively with granular matter or pure mechanics, it can get along as well or better within their limits without extraneous considerations, just as practical mechanics can ignore the changes in mass which occur at speeds near that of light. But science as a whole, if it is not to exist divided into walled-up compartments, must attempt to synthesize its understanding of reality. As Teilhard says in *Comment je crois,* the illusion of the materialists is to consider the elements of analysis as more real than the products of synthesis. However, "it is not in their germinal state that beings manifest themselves but in their florescence." [41]

If we link the sciences in ascending order of the complex unity of their special objects from physics through chemistry, biology, anthropology, to the social and psychological sciences, we find that the former are more exact, their symbol system more abstract and mathematical, and their emotional component is low. As we move up the scale, the human element, freedom, and emotional factors increase while the exactitude and degree of abstraction diminish. Yet all are attempting to know, to understand, and to increase man's control over the same undivided reality. Each department of science has a method appropriate to its field, but science would only be imitating the quarrel of the blind men over the elephant if each of its departments were to impose the strictures of its own method upon science as a whole. Indeed, the results produced by each discipline can never be fully understood unless they can be related synthetically with all others. But synthetic reasoning leads directly to philosophy. "The future of knowledge . . . As a first approximation it is outlined on our horizon as the establishment of an overall and completely coherent perspective of the universe." [42] The goal is eschatological but it is also a present guide to our endeavor.

For Teilhard, however, scientifically informed philosophy is not to be confused with what he often rejects as "metaphys-

ics," the attempt to deduce the world from an *a priori* definition of being. "To philosophize," for Teilhard, "is to organize
the lines of reality around us." In contrast to the Socratic
method of bringing out in dialogue that latent "recollection" of
the eternal truth which each soul brings with it from its source,
in contrast to scholastic reasoning from self-evident proposi-
tions, Teilhard's method is to start with the most simple and
elementary objects of science and to build up synthetically
and dialectically from them a "hyperphysics," not a metaphysics.[43] For, as he says, "Every formal abstraction tends to pronounce judgment, perhaps prematurely, on the ambiguity of
the future. It risks fixing the movement when it is from the
movement itself that the desired synthesis will emerge." [44]

But Teilhard also has his *a priori* assumptions. He says,
"Is it not the peculiar difficulty of every synthesis that its end
is already implicit in its beginnings?" Two such assumptions
he carefully notes in *The Phenomenon of Man,* "Two basic
assumptions: the primacy accorded to the psychic and to
thought in the stuff of the universe . . . and the 'biological'
value attributed to the social fact around us." [45] Here, I believe, Teilhard is hiding his trumps. His two premises actually
stem from a single one, which he saves for the end of his argument—his Christian faith. The real difference between Teilhard's method and rational metaphysics is that where the
philosopher's *a priori* principles are thought to be innate in
man's reason or in the physical universe, Teilhard's are eschatological and given to man through God's self-revelation in
Christ to faith. We shall return to this ultimately decisive
point at the end of our discussion.

THE LANGUAGE OF ANALOGY

Our study of analysis and synthesis leads us into the field
of language and symbols, to which so many philosophers

have devoted their major energies in the last generation, and which has been the subject of so much discussion and controversy among theologians that I can hardly begin to summarize it.[46] As we have seen, the physical and analytical sciences investigate nature by tracing everything back to its simplest and most discrete elements. It was thought for a while that language could be analyzed in the same way, tying its symbols to concrete and empirically identifiable objects or relating them by a logic like that of geometry. But in the meanwhile science itself, in its very pursuit of the basic elements of matter, lost its direct empirical contact with its objects. Matter, as it divided itself into finer and finer elements under the scientist's scalpel, lost its tangible consistency and evaporated into a haze of vibrations, energy quanta, and ephemeral "particles" whose nature and very existence could be postulated only by the most sophisticated interpretation of indirect evidence of their activity, until finally a limit to positive measurement was reached with Heisenberg's principle of uncertainty. "For modern natural science," Heisenberg said, "there is no longer in the beginning the material object, but form, mathematical symmetry. And since mathematical structure is in the last analysis an intellectual content, we could say, in the words of Goethe's Faust, 'in the beginning was the word'—the logos." [47]

"Everything—*really everything*—is simultaneously particle and field," says Erwin Schrödinger; and further on, "Real existence is a term undoubtedly almost hunted down by many philosophical hounds, and its simple, naïve meaning has almost been lost to us." [48]

Science itself has pulled the rug out from under the whole movement to define and limit the meaning of language by tying it to the narrow framework of positivistic science and abstract mathematics. And ever since Wittgenstein renounced the dogmas of his *Tractatus Logico-Philosophicus,* and the publication of his posthumous *Philosophical Investigations,* the tide in philosophy appears to have turned.

There is no use beating a dead horse; but the prejudices, the illiteracy, the general inability to interpret or to understand poetic language, unfortunately lingers on. How many men and women have not grown up intellectually starved by a pinched educational diet restricted to the "facts" recognized by a dry and narrow mechanical view of this unimaginably rich and mysterious universe of ours? To how many are not the great poetic visions of genius, not to speak of the marvelously expressive imagery of the Bible, simply incomprehensible for lack of any training in the poetic idiom? Little wonder that recent attempts to "demythologize" theological language and translate it into a debased tongue succeed only in reducing the Christian message to their least common denominator.

The problem to which linguistic analysis addressed itself, however, remains: how to distinguish between language which refers truthfully to a generally recognized world, and fallacies, individual illusions, and irrational outbursts of private emotion. The strait jacket of univocal reference to discrete objects, as we have seen, confines language to a narrow range of our experience of reality. The heart of the problem is that reality, while basically one continuum, is at the same time manifest on a number of different levels. The dialectic of synthesis, Teilhard has shown us, carries the stuff of the universe over a ladder of thresholds, at each of which new qualities emerge which were invisible before and yet latent, waiting only their union in a "critical mass" to explode into view. There are hence qualitative differences between levels yet a fundamental continuity. The very qualities in the lower elements which carry them toward the higher are revealed only *after* their emergence through synthesis. So we can understand fully the lower only by reference to the higher.

Only in man, for instance, does consciousness and freedom

emerge perceptibly to us. Only in man does the "within" of things become an object of direct intuition, Teilhard points out. But, "since the stuff of the universe has an inner aspect at one point of itself, there is necessarily a *double aspect to its structure*." [49] Speaking as a scientist, Pierre Auger points to a parallel concept: "The similarity of structure between this world and our thinking . . . a sound foundation for a kind of monism [to] save us from the threat of intellectual schizophrenia that the absolute separation between the world of things and that of spirit constantly holds over us." "This liaison was made possible," he goes on to say, "only after a reflective study of his own internal structure by man himself." [50]

Nature henceforth can only be fully understood as that which has produced mind and, conversely, can be known only in terms of the rational patterns by which mind organizes its perceptions of nature. "It blends itself with the soul's potentialities," says Teilhard, "to such an extent that soon the soul no longer knows how to distinguish space-time from its own thoughts." [51] Man stands at the peak of evolution where, for him at least, its lines converge. That is his viewpoint; he can have no other. Looking at the world as a whole he may divide it into discrete compartments, each with its own properties and laws—inanimate matter, plant and animal life, humanity and the "supernatural"—and deny any real connection between them. In this case each division will have its own local language. Or, and this is what Teilhard is proposing, he may try to see each level as part of one whole, and, while keeping their differences in mind, he may develop a language capable of expressing their unity in relationship.

This language is a language of analogy. Since man has direct experience of mind, purpose, freedom, love, etc., only within himself, he can apply such terms univocally only to other human beings. To levels below or above his own they can be applied only by means of analogy whose distinctive merit is to respect *both* the continuity *and* the discontinuity between the two levels which it links. Teilhard's language is replete with analogies—speaking of society as analogous to an organism for example—but he is aware of their dangers also. "How can we assure the correct application of the analogy?" he asks, "that is, how can we go beyond the metaphor without falling into the ridiculous and simple-minded identification of humanity with some kind of a great, living beast?" [52] A true analogy may be misconstrued in either of two directions, by ignoring the qualitative threshold between its two terms, or by rejecting the reality of their similarities.

The real problem, once the proper function of analogy is understood, is to find the best analogy for the universe. The analogy of a machine is obviously inadequate for a world-process which has produced man, and besides, we cannot even conceive of a machine without reference to its purpose—and purpose brings us up to the human level. The analogy of a complex, self-directing organism is better, but here again we "know" the inner life of animals only by analogy to our own personal experience. Finally, and inescapably, the only adequate analogy by which we can think and speak about nature as a whole is that of mind.[53] Even the most positivistic scientists resort to metaphors which can only refer to mind, but they do so surreptitiously, the reference hidden in their language, as when one might say, "matter is groping toward more complex arrangements." Or, to be less obvious, let us quote from a textbook definition: "Crystallization is the spontaneous arrangement of molecules into a repetitive, orderly array." Both "spontaneous" and "orderly" are words which refer to the human mind. "Order" is a quality of the mind and only mind can distinguish its pattern from any other random arrangement. In doing so it makes a value judgment, implicitly judging one crystal to be more perfect than another.[54]

If, on the other hand, we accept the analogy of the world in its totality to mind, openly but with caution, everything changes. We men are no longer isolated in a strange, cold universe of matter which dissolves into more and more abstract mathematical symbols the more we try to understand it. Instead it becomes the purposeful, creative womb, which brought us into being, waiting only for our maturity to be understood, ready to reveal itself to our persistent inquiry. It gives us at last a unified image of the universe within which the irreducible opposites of analytical reasoning are resolved by the synthetic ascent of matter-spirit. We are on our way toward a *personal universe,* a universe which, as Teilhard says, "comes out of shadows, is no longer a senseless prison: it becomes comprehensible and takes on value, leaves room for liberty, and demands our love." [55]

But we are jumping ahead. So far we have spoken mainly of the attempt to understand the lower by analogy to the human mind. But the individual mind is not the ultimate. It is only a part of an as yet unfinished creation. If we are to grow toward an understanding of the whole complex, ourselves and the world together, we must look higher up the ladder of synthesis and into the future, toward the unknown. "Here only, at this turning point where the future substitutes itself for the present and the observations of science should give way to the anticipations of faith, do our perplexities legitimately, and indeed inevitably, begin." [56]

For our efforts to discover the perfect paradigm by which to illuminate and unite our concept of reality cannot stop at the analogy of mind in its merely rational and orderly sense, as the Deists did. Even to see a personal God as creator and goal of the universe is not enough. Everything depends upon what kind of "person" (or rather, "hyper-person") God is: a cosmic engineer? a vengeful tyrant? Are we his slaves, his darlings, or his playthings? Our whole outlook will depend on how we answer.

For the totality of the cosmos in time-space, its goal and its purpose, can be fully understood, and its antinomies thereby resolved, only when it is seen from its end and summit where all its lines finally converge. In other words, our universe can be *completely* known only from the point of view of God. So our situation is now reversed. Instead of trying to comprehend the lower by analogy with ourselves, we must try to find analogies which will open our understanding to that which is on a qualitatively higher level than our own. And here the risk is no longer to attribute too much to the lower, but to fail in attributing enough to the higher. The parables of Jesus are just such analogies, and the sentimentalized image of Jesus in so many minds is the result of failing to interpret them as such.

But rightly understood, Jesus is, in one of his aspects, the human analogy of God, the revelation to us, on our level, of the mind, the freedom, the sacrificial love, the supra-personal unity which are the ultimate qualities of the cosmos, but, which apart from Jesus, can manifest themselves to us fully and empirically only when the world's synthetic process is complete at Christ's Parousia. "For now I know in part; then I shall understand fully, even as I have been fully understood" (I Cor. 13:12).

Theology attempts to speak truthfully about the universe understood in its relation to the whole—its purpose, its end, its summit—in other words, as God's continuous creation. It must do so by analogy, respecting always the qualitative discontinuity between its levels.[57] And, as Teilhard has repeatedly pointed out, humanity's ascent toward greater consciousness, freedom, and unity cannot continue without both a vision of its supra-personal goal and a zeal to attain to it:

"From this point of view, intellectual discovery and synthesis are no longer mere speculation but creation." [58]

THE CONJUNCTION OF SCIENCE AND MYSTICISM

Thus, there are two paths to knowledge of the higher: extrapolation of the past and ongoing process, and God's self-revelation. Teilhard's plan is to join these two ladders, the one extended from below, the other lowered from above, into one Jacob's ladder between earth and heaven. And this feat is possible only insofar as they are both sustained by the same faith.

Extrapolation, especially of a process in which freedom is increasingly operative, is risky and speculative. Scientists are quite right to be wary of it. And, as Teilhard himself says, in *Le Christique*:

In the end, no matter how much we may be persuaded . . . that a superior pole of completion and consolidation (call it Omega) awaits us at the consummation of hominization, this pole, Omega, is actually known only by extrapolation and remains merely postulated and conjectural. . . . But what happens if, on the other hand, our spirit awakens, first to the possibility, then to the evidence that the Christ of Revelation is none other than the Omega of evolution? Then, all at once, the empirical universe becomes, before our eyes and in our heart, at last coherent and purposeful.[59]

The failure of the metaphysicians and their pantheistic tendencies show us our crying need for God's revelation of himself.[60] There is a point beyond which all our efforts, no matter how brilliant, beautiful, or well informed, become lost in fragile, abstract, unconvincing speculation. We can raise our ladders only so far without hooking on to some firm support from above. The tower of Babel led only to the confusion of tongues. To open ourselves to reality, we must not only quest for it but also submit ourselves wholly to its revealing power and, like the great discoverers in art and science, alternate between intensive effort and receptive contemplation, such as Teilhard practiced in the Ignatian exercises.

"In short," says Teilhard, reviewing his whole method, "as soon as science outgrows the analytic investigations which constitute its lower and preliminary stages, and passes on to synthesis—synthesis which naturally culminates in the realization of some superior state of humanity—it is at once led to foresee and place its stakes on the *future* and on the *all*. And with that it out-distances itself and emerges in terms of *option* and *adoration*"—that is to say, religion, "the conjunction of reason and mysticism." [61]

For Teilhard, mysticism is living in the Divine Milieu, seeing the oneness of all things, referring everything to the whole, sensing the omnipresence of God, founding one's faith on his self-revelation, being in communion with Christ. "He who dares to believe," Teilhard affirms, "enters a sphere in which all created things, while keeping their habitual textures," like the elements of the Eucharist, "seem to be made of another substance. All phenomena remain the same in themselves and yet all become luminous, living and loving. . . . By the power of faith, it is Christ himself who appears, emerging, yet violating nothing, at the heart of the world." [62]

"Beautiful!" some of his readers may exclaim; or even, "Agreed! But how is this passionate and illuminating faith acquired?" That is the key question. For, as Teilhard tells us in *Comment je crois,* faith grows in our spirits by weaving around itself a coherent network of thoughts and actions. But this network grows and ultimately holds together only under the organizing power of the *initial faith* whose origin is ineffable. If for a moment it fails, the whole structure and vision collapses with it. The world becomes, for that moment, absurd. "[Faith] cannot, therefore, be obtained directly by any reasoning or by any human artifice. Like life itself . . . it is a gift." [63]

All Teilhard's arguments, then, all his scientific evidence and reasonings put together, amount to no more—and no less— than "an education of our eyes." There is no proof, no evidence that can compel unwilling belief; "there are only rational invitations to an act of faith." Reason cannot give birth to faith; on the other hand, we cannot long cling to a faith which we are unable to justify intellectually. [64]

Teilhard's education of our eyes also has another and complementary function, namely, to clear away the scales of prejudice and to loosen the blinders which limit our vision to the field of yesterday's science or divide it into two unrelated spheres. In the famous words from Blake's *Marriage of Heaven and Hell:* "If the doors of perception were cleansed everything would appear to man as it is, infinite. For man has closed himself up till he sees all things thro' narrow chinks of his cavern."

Faith is a gift which, for all Teilhard's passionate desire to communicate, is not his to give. When he has done all he can to open our eyes, he can only point to the means of grace which God has provided. For faith, like the love from which it is inseparable, cannot be learned from books alone. It must be lived, practiced, tested in community with others. And if any man desires this gift-without-price, let him begin by placing himself in that community whose life it is. Let him open himself to the Bible's prophetic vision of a world centered on God, to the Evangelist's witness to God's Word Incarnate, and to Saint Paul's faith in the risen Christ: "the image of the invisible God, the first-born of all creation," in whom "all things hold together" (Col. 1:15f.). Let him prepare himself to meet Christ, to offer himself and to become one with him in his holy Eucharist. These are the principal, if not the only, means of grace which God himself has given us.

For (and wherever we begin to follow Teilhard he will always lead us to the same conclusion), "His prevenient grace is always ready to inspire our first look and our first prayer. Ultimately the initiative, the awakening, comes always from Him, and whatever the subsequent growth of our mystic faculties, no progress can be made except through renewed response to new gifts. . . . So we are led to depend for our incorporation into the Divine Milieu on an intense and unceasing prayer—supplication for the fundamental gift: *Domine, fac ut videam.*" [65]

"What my mouth cannot communicate to my brothers and sisters, [Christ] will tell them better than I," Teilhard wrote in the midst of the First World War.

That which my heart desires for them with such anxious and helpless ardor, he will give to them if he thinks it good. That which men cannot hear through my feeble voice, that to which they stop their ears in order not to hear, I can alway confide to Christ who will repeat it one day to their hearts. Knowing this, I can die happily with my ideal and be buried with the vision which I so hoped to share with others. Christ gathers up for the life of the future all our smothered ambitions, partial insights, unfinished or clumsy efforts, if they be sincere. *Nunc dimittis, Domine, servum tuum in pace* . . .[66]

—and to complete Father Teilhard's citation—

For mine eyes have seen thy salvation.

Author's Notes

INTRODUCTION: TEILHARD AND HIS GENERATION

1. Jacques Chastenet, *Histoire de la Troisième République* (Paris: Hachette, 1960), Vol. I, Ch. VIII.

2. *Ibid.,* Vol. II, Ch. IV.

3. P. Leroy, Introduction to *Letters from a Traveller* (New York: Harper & Bros., 1962), p. 20. Hereafter abbreviated *LT*. C. Cuénot, *P. Teilhard de Chardin, Les Grandes Etapes de son Evolution* (Paris: Plon, 1958), p. 13, fn. Cuénot's is the most complete biography of Teilhard to date. He also presents large extracts from his works and letters in their chronological development, and the most complete bibliography of Teilhard's many articles and essays.

4. Cuénot, p. 28f.

5. *Ibid.,* p. 17.

6. Chastenet, Vol. III, Chs. X, XI.

7. See Charles E. Raven, *Teilhard de Chardin, Scientist and Seer* (New York: Harper & Row, 1962), Ch. III.

8. Francisco de Suarez, Spanish, Jesuit, theologian, 1548-1617, advocate of Congruism.

9. P. Smulders, *La Vision de Teilhard de Chardin* (Paris: Desclée de Brouwer, 1964), p. 126, fn. Father Smulders, a specialist in patristics and history of doctrine, is Professor at the Jesuit Seminary at Maastricht, Holland.

10. Cf. Cuénot, p. 25, Raven, p. 46, Henri de Lubac, S.J., *La Pensée religieuse du Père Teilhard de Chardin* (Paris: Aubier, 1962), p. 80f. H. de Lubac is one of the leading modern and reforming theologians of France. His many works range from exegesis and ecclesiology to modern philosophy and oriental religions.

11. Georges Crespy, *La Pensée Théologique de Teilhard de Chardin* (Paris: Eds. Universitaires, 1961), p. 66. G. Crespy is Professor of Theology at the Protestant Seminary of Montpellier, France.

12. See Cuénot's Bibliography; *Le prêtre,* quoted by Cuénot, p. 44, See also *Genèse d'une pensée, Lettres de 1914 à 1919* (Paris: Grasset, 1961).

13. Cuénot, p. 71.

14. Cuénot, p. 85; Smulders, p. 18.

15. Cuénot, p. 150; Smulders, p. 19; *LT*, p. 159.

16. *LT*, p. 301; see also pp. 41, 134, 232, 337.

17. Cuénot, p. 325; see also *LT*, pp. 240, 242.

18. Also known as Peking man.

19. "It will be 1925 over again, with New York instead of China. The only thing is, I'm seventy. . . . Even so, it may be, once more, an intervention of Providence, and the opening up of a new field." *LT*, p. 320.

20. See, among others, Robert T. Francoeur, ed., *The World of Teilhard de Chardin* (Baltimore: Helicon, 1961); C. E. Raven, *op. cit.*; N. Braybrooke, ed., *Teilhard de Chardin, Pilgrim of the Future* (New York: Seabury, 1964); Helmut de Terra, *Memories of Teilhard de Chardin* (New York: Harper & Row, 1964); and the Introductions to *The Phenomenon of Man* by Julian Huxley and to *Letters from a Traveller* by Pierre Leroy, S.J.

CHAPTER 1: WORLD, MIND, AND SPIRIT

1. *The Phenomenon of Man*, trans. B. Wall (New York: Harper & Row, 1959), p. 29. *Le Phénomène Humain*, 1947 (Paris: Editions du Seuil, 1955). Hereafter abbreviated *PoM*. Page references are to New York edition.

2. *PoM*, p. 39.

3. *Ibid.*, p. 47, cf. fn.

4. *Ibid.*, p. 134f.

5. *Ibid.*, pp. 48, 61, and passim.

6. We shall see that Teilhard's thesis gains much support from the fact that man has succeeded in harnessing the energy of nuclear fission under conditions where it was classically considered as unavailable; but there is a theoretical limit even to that.

7. An alternative, the Constant State theorem, envisages an indefinitely self-sustaining universe, but within it, all complex structures decay, like trees in a forest, only to be replaced by new ones, so that the whole is everlastingly similar, thus likewise denying any ultimate value to evolution.

8. *PoM*, pp. 52ff.

9. *Ibid.*, pp. 62ff.

10. *The Future of Man*, trans. N. Denny (New York: Harper & Row, 1964). This editorial title covers twenty-two essays from 1920 to 1955. Citations and page references are to *L'Avenir de l'Homme* (Paris: Seuil, 1959). References to the New York edition follow in parentheses. Hereafter abbreviated *FoM*. See p. 268 (209).

11. *PoM*, p. 55.

12. *Ibid.*, pp. 58ff.

13. *Ibid.*, p. 62.

14. *Ibid.*, p. 61; *FoM*, pp. 116f. (88f.), 268 (209).

15. *PoM*, p. 142f.

16. *Ibid.*, p. 53.

17. Michael Polanyi, *Personal Knowledge* (Univ. of Chicago Press, 1958), p. 39. Gives several vivid examples of this principle at work.

18. English in the original.

19. Letter of Feb. 27, 1953, quoted in Cuénot, p. 368.

20. *PoM*, p. 110f.

21. *Ibid.*, p. 34. Teilhard is criticized by modern biologists for holding Lamarckian views of evolution by inheritance of teleologically adaptive and inventive characteristics. In fact he attempts to make a synthesis of the Lamarckian and Darwinian view (external natural selection of chance mutations). The "within" works purposively, the "without" by external causality. Since the "within" emerges fully only with human consciousness, the Lamarckian factor is scarcely detectable below that threshold. The subject is too complex for full discussion here, but we should point out that Teilhard's conclusions as to the direction of evolution need not hang upon his Lamarckian leanings since he sees the operation of Providence in *all* the factors of the total situation, or, as we have pointed out, as an organizing field which creatively finalizes random groping. For a fuller discussion, see P. F. Forsthoefel, S.J., in Francoeur, pp. 98ff. and Polanyi, pp. 33ff. and 382ff.

22. Actually with respect to size, man stands about halfway between the immense and the infinitesimal, but we have already seen that in matter's synthetic ascent, only a tiny fraction reaches the higher levels; so it is natural that man should bulk small in the cosmos.

23. *PoM*, p. 34. Teilhard also recognizes the possibility of other inhabited planets with whose cultures man may one day establish contact, but in the absence of empirical evidence he leaves this eventuality aside, for it in no way contradicts his main argument. See *PoM*, p. 286.

24. *Ibid.*, p. 276; *FoM*, p. 91f. (67). Teilhard's "neo-anthropocentrism."

25. *PoM*, p. 148. But does not contradict its methods and results within their proper limits.

26. *Ibid.*, pp. 164ff.

27. *Ibid.*, p. 166f. The concept of critical thresholds of continuity-discontinuity is another of Teilhard's fundamental principles, by which he unites dynamically the classical antinomies of philosophy. We shall have occasion to return to it later.

28. *Ibid.*, p. 202.

29. *Ibid.*, p. 152.

30. Leaps from one realm to another, analogous to those performed in the changes of structure and energy of matter according to quantum laws; a result of the basically granular nature of matter-energy.

31. True socialization, involving diversity and specialization as distinguished from mere colonization, symbiosis, parasitism, etc. *PoM,* p. 154.

32. *PoM,* p. 208.

33. *Ibid.*, p. 224.

34. *Ibid.*, p. 246.

35. Cuénot, p. 80.

36. *PoM,* p. 251.

37. *Ibid.*, p. 232; cf. Polanyi, p. 266.

38. See *La grande option* (1939) in *FoM,* p. 57 (37); also p. 331 (254).

39. *PoM,* p. 256.

40. *Ibid.*, p. 264f.

41. *FoM,* p. 65 (45).

42. *PoM,* p. 251f. Note that Tillich uses the same linguistic device, the supra-personal, to designate God whom we cannot describe univocally in terms of present experience. "The depth of being cannot be symbolized by objects taken from the realm of things or sub-personal living beings. The supra-personal is not an 'It,' or more exactly, it is a 'He' as much as it is an 'It' and it is above both of them." *Theology of Culture* (New York: Oxford, 1959), p. 131.

43. *PoM,* pp. 267ff.

44. *Ibid.*, p. 261f.

45. *Ibid.*, p. 269.

46. *Ibid.*, p. 287.

CHAPTER 2: CHRIST AND THE COSMOS

1. *Hymn of the Universe,* p. 36 (36). Editorial title covers *The Mass on the World* (1923), *Christ in the World of Matter* (1916), *The Spiritual Power of Matter* (1919), and excerpts from many other essays. Hereafter abbreviated *HU*. Citations and references are to *Hymne de l'Univers* (Paris: Seuil, 1961). References to the New York edition follow in parentheses.

2. Cuénot, p. 262.

3. *Le Christique* (1955), cited in Crespy, p. 70.

4. The healthy organism already accomplishes this within the limits of its life span, its mind surviving a number of material renewals of its body.

5. *PoM*, p. 267.

6. *FoM*, p. 227 (179f.); *PoM*, pp. 254ff.

7. E.g., *PoM*, p. 294.

8. *FoM*, p. 404 (309).

9. *Ibid.*, p. 153 (120).

10. Quoted in *HU*, p. 84 (80).

11. The originistic fallacy.

12. *PoM*, p. 272.

13. *FoM*, p. 285 (223).

14. *The Divine Milieu* (1926) (New York: Harper & Row, 1960), p. 140 (94). Hereafter abbreviated *DM*. Citations and references are from *Le Milieu Divin* (Paris: Seuil, 1957). References to the New York edition follow in parentheses.

15. As Teilhard entitles an essay of 1939, *FoM*, pp. 55ff. (37ff.).

16. P. Tillich, *Systematic Theology* (Univ. of Chicago Press), Vol. I, Introduction.

17. A contribution, that is, to the theology which has become traditional since the adoption of Platonic and Aristotelian categories in the Middle Ages, for it can be argued that the temporal dimension of science itself is largely of Judaeo-Christian origin. See, e.g., Thorleif Boman, *Hebrew Thought Compared with Greek* (S.C.M. Press, 1960).

18. See *FoM*, pp. 78ff. (57ff.) and 118ff. (89ff.), and C. Tresmontant, *Pierre Teilhard de Chardin, His Thought* (Baltimore: Helicon Press, 1959), p. 18.

19. E.g., *FoM*, pp. 116 (88) and 286 (224), and the letters of 1954 quoted by Cuénot, pp. 441 and 449. Here Teilhard stands Plato on his head, as it were: the world of becoming is a present reality rather than that of ideal forms. But Teilhard preserves the Platonic idealism none the less by transposing it onto the scale of time. He transcends the dispute between realists and nominalists by treating particulars as present realities and ideal forms as eschatological realities which are in continuous dynamic relationship.

20. *FoM*, p. 111 (83). The "Cone of Time" is a convenient term to designate the convergent universe, not at any one stage of its existence but in the totality of its entire history, somewhat as we might speak of "the life of Lincoln" as a single entity in space and time as distinguished from Lincoln, the man, at any given moment.

21. *PoM*, p. 284.

22. *LT*, p. 296.

23. *L'Esquisse d'un univers personnel* (1936), quoted in Crespy, p. 59. See also *Mon Univers*, cited by H. de Lubac, p. 282, fn.: "absolute multiplicity is synonymous with nonentity."

24. *PoM*, p. 271.

25. *Ibid.*, p. 271.

26. *LT*, p. 151.

27. E. Jacob, *Theology of the Old Testament* (New York: Harper & Row, 1958), p. 317.

28. *La Vision du Passé* (Paris: Seuil, 1957), p. 323.

29. *FoM*, p. 378 (290); see also p. 256f. (199f.).

30. *HU*, p. 21f. (22).

31. *PoM*, p. 53.

32. *Ibid.*, p. 57.

33. *HU*, p. 107 (100).

34. *Ibid.*, p. 21 (22).

35. *PoM*, p. 264f.

36. *FoM*, p. 121f. (91f.).

37. Cf. Tresmontant, p. 94.

38. *HU*, p. 20f. (21).

39. *Le Christ dans la matière* (1919) in *HU*, p. 57 (54).

40. *La sainte evolution,* from *La vie cosmique* (1916), quoted in Cuénot, p. 53. Here we can see that Teilhard's concept of God does not oppose, but encompasses the existentialist's "Depth of Being." See also *LT*, p. 66. In *Comment je crois,* Teilhard tells us that God is "hidden," not because he wishes to leave us in ignorance and suffering, but because *we men* and our universe are not yet sufficiently evolved (organized) to be able to support an unveiled Epiphany. Hence the humble "kenosis" of God's Word in Jesus Christ. See Exod. 33:20 and Phil. 2:5ff.

41. *FoM*, p. 396 (304).

42. *PoM*, p. 308.

43. *FoM*, p. 403 (308).

44. *FoM*, p. 25 (12).

45. *DM*, p. 45 (27).

46. *FoM*, p. 31 (18).

47. *HU*, p. 81f. (77).

48. Cf. I Cor. 15:45-50, especially: "Just as we have borne the image of the man of dust, we shall also bear the image of the man of heaven." This inability to know our own proper nature until we encounter and accept Jesus Christ is the "estrangement from self" stressed by the existential theologians and which can be healed by faith in Christ, the bearer of our "new being," in Tillich's term.

49. *Le milieu mystique* (1917) in *HU*, p. 128 (118).

50. *Mon univers* (1924), *HU*, p. 80 (76).

51. *La vie cosmique* (1916), *FoM*, p. 396f. (304f.).

52. *FoM*, p. 152 (120).

53. *PoM*, p. 267.

54. The "scandal" stressed by Tertullian, Kierkegaard, and

their successors, the paradox of the Incarnation whereby the eternal transcendent God enters into history in the form of an individual, is indeed somewhat attenuated when, with the early Apologists and Greek Fathers, the divine in Christ is identified with the Logos, the Creative Word of God who has been instrumental, active, and immanent in Nature and History from the beginning. There remains undiminished, however, the paradox of his humility, incognito, and suffering, of which Teilhard makes much. See Jacob, pp. 127ff., for the Old Testament theology of the Creative Word or Wisdom and his hypostatization in prophecy. See A. Richardson, *An Introduction to the Theology of the New Testament* (New York: Harper & Row, 1958), pp. 155ff., for its relation to Christ.

55. O. Cullmann, *Christ and Time* (Phila.: Westminster, 1950).

56. *DM*, p. 140f. (94).

57. Teilhard often uses the word *amorizer* in similar contexts.

58. *Esquisse d'un univers personnel* (1936), cited in Cuénot, p. 239. A similar emphasis on the risen, cosmic Christ, the Pantocrator of the Greek Fathers, has been preserved in the art and liturgy of the Orthodox Churches, while in the West, the focus came to be mainly on Christ crucified because of the stress on sin and penance.

59. *DM*, p. 49 (30).

60. *La vie cosmique* (1916), *HU*, p. 156 (144). Cf. Col. 1-2; Phil. 2:9ff.

61. Letter of 1954, cited by Cuénot, p. 441.

62. *HU*, p. 23 (24).

63. *DM*, p. 128 (86).

64. *Ibid.*, pp. 117 (77f.), 153 (103).

65. Smulders, p. 234.

66. This touches upon one of the major points of cleavage between contemporary theologians. For the school of "realized eschatology," faith saves a man "in the moment" by his personal appropriation of an act of God which translates him from servitude to time into an "eternal now." For this school, secular history is largely indifferent to salvation, which is seen mainly in terms of the individual's response to the Gospel. Teilhard, on the other hand, stands with that school which sees salvation as fully realized only through and beyond a collective historical process. Common to both schools, however, is the affirmation that in the cross and resurrection of Christ, salvation is assured to faith *now,* and that the act of God necessary to ultimate success has been accomplished. In this sense, all would agree that the world's redemption was performed on the cross.

67. *DM*, p. 197f. (135).

68. *La vie cosmique* (1916), *HU*, p. 144 (133).

69. See *PoM*, p. 291; *FoM*, p. 155 (122); *DM*, p. 149 (100f.). "And I, when I am lifted up from the earth, will draw all men to myself" (John 12:32).

70. The principle of election is also operative throughout Teilhard's system. Just as a particular portion of matter is "chosen" to partake of each upward step in evolution in order that the whole cosmos may be raised to a higher level of organization, so one particular branch of the mammals emerged into manhood, and one nation became God's chosen people through the agency of a single chosen prophet. In each case that which is chosen and carried into higher being has the concomitant mission of saving the remainder. Israel was to be a light to the nations, not an end unto herself. The principle narrows down finally to the supreme example of God's elect in Jesus Christ, who undergoes in the form of a servant the sacrificial progress through death and resurrection by which the whole of God's people is to be raised to eternal life in him. It follows that the Church of the elect is not a place where the saints are released from the world and rewarded, but a community whose mission is to act as God's agent in the world's salvation.

71. *Comment je vois* (1948), cited in Smulders, p. 252.

72. Letter, *circa* 1948?, cited in Cuénot, p. 372.

73. *FoM*, p. 53 (36), and letter of 1951, cited in Cuénot, p. 446.

74. *FoM*, p. 35 (23).

75. *LT*, p. 127.

76. *HU*, p. 30 (31).

77. *PoM*, p. 273.

78. *Ibid.*, p. 291.

79. *FoM*, p. 347 (267), and Eph. 4:11f.

80. *FoM*, p. 156 (123), and Rom. 7:24.

81. *FoM*, p. 70 (50).

82. *Ibid.*, pp. 402 (307) and 384 (295).

83. *DM*, p. 164 (111).

84. See *FoM*, p. 348 (268), and fn.

85. *DM*, p. 200 (137).

86. *FoM*, p. 76 (55). See also *HU*, p. 129f. (119f.).

87. *DM*, p. 181 (124).

88. *Ibid.*, p. 139 (93f.).

CHAPTER 3: THE CHRISTIAN LIFE

1. *Messe sur le monde, HU*, p. 29 (29).

2. The same may be said of the Kings of Israel, of the expected Messianic King, and of Christ as Son of David.

3. See especially John 15:1-6, "I am the true vine . . . you are the branches," etc., the vine being an Old Testament image of Israel (e.g., Ps. 80:8, Jer. 2:21, Isa. 5:1-7).

4. It must be admitted that the New Testament, and indeed Paul himself, uses "world" ambiguously: in one sense, the world is being saved, in another it must be left behind in order to be saved (e.g., I Cor. 2:12; John 15:19, 17:6; Jas. 1:27, 4:4). And we shall find the same distinction in Teilhard. But this is an ambiguity, not an antinomy, for the Gospel is "turning the world upside down" (Acts 17:6), that is, it is both carrying it over a threshold to an entirely new quality of life, and also transforming the believer's view of it; hence "world" may refer either to the old, unredeemed milieu out of which Christ is causing us to emerge, or to the entire historical process moving toward union with Christ who both overcomes the world and saves it (John 4:42 and 16:33). Note that in I Cor. 7:31 it is the "form" (Gk., *schema*) of this world that is passing away, not the world itself.

5. *LT*, p. 228.

6. *DM*, pp. 45f. (27), 124f. (82f.).

7. *PoM*, p. 111.

8. *FoM*, p. 283 (221).

9. *DM*, p. 58 (36).

10. *FoM*, p. 120 (91).

11. *PoM*, p. 259.

12. *Comment je vois*, cited in Crespy, p. 113.

13. *FoM*, p. 288 (225).

14. "The real man is the man who gathers, or will gather, within himself the consciousness of the whole human stratum" (*LT*, p. 133). Only Christ, or one who is "in Christ" is fully a man by this definition.

15. Letter of 1930, *LT*, p. 164.

16. *FoM*, p. 169 (133).

17. *PoM*, p. 263.

18. *Ibid.*, p. 263.

19. *Ibid.*, p. 266.

20. We should note that the natural, psycho-biological forces in man are not themselves evil or sinful. Sin lies in turning back in attachment to them rather than striving ahead toward growth, spirit, and God (Phil. 3:12f.).

21. C.F.D. Moule's translation in the *Cambridge Greek Testament Commentary*, Colossians, p. 100f.

22. *FoM*, p. 270 (211).

23. *HU*, p. 21 (21) and *FoM*, p. 305 (237).

24. *DM*, p. 179 (122).

25. *FoM*, p. 63f. (43f.); Cuénot, pp. 175 and 359f.

26. Letter of 1951, cited in Cuénot, p. 316.

27. *FoM*, p. 104 (79).

28. This must, of course, be understood in the light of God's grace working through man's faculties. The relation is beautifully stated in the phrase cited earlier: "For the creature must work if he wishes to be further created."

29. *DM*, p. 48f. (30).

30. *Ibid.*, p. 125f. (83).

31. *Ibid.*, p. 57 (36).

32. *Ibid.*, p. 57 (36). Cf. Luther: "The sphere of faith's works is worldly society and its order" (*Address to the German Nobility*).

33. Letter of 1930, *LT*, p. 164.

34. *DM*, p. 50 (30).

35. *Ibid.*, pp. 51 (31), 56 (35).

36. *Ibid.*, p. 125 (84). To cling on or to turn back is sin. To press on is virtue, as Saint Paul tells us in the third chapter of Philippians, which should be read as a whole in this connection, especially where he says that he has not yet attained to perfection in Christ, "but one thing I do, forgetting what lies behind and straining forward to what lies ahead, I press on toward the goal for the prize of the upward call of God in Christ Jesus" (Phil. 3:13bf.). Cf. Luke 9:62, "No man, having put his hand to the plough and looking back, is fit for the Kingdom of God."

37. *HU*, p. 27 (28).

38. *DM*, p. 175 (119).

39. See *ibid.*, pp. 55 (34) and 100 (65).

40. *HU*, p. 138f. (128).

41. *Ibid.*, p. 67 (64).

42. 1918, *HU*, pp. 61ff. (59).

43. Matter is of course taken in its largest possible sense: "I am the fire that burns, the waters that sweep away—the love which initiates and the truth which passes. Everything which imposes itself, which renews, which unleashes and which unites: Force, Experience, Progress, Matter—I am all this" (*HU*, p. 63 (61). Matter, in Teilhard's vocabulary, is almost synonymous with what is broadly called History, and must not be confused with matter as it is "described, reduced, or disfigured by the pontiffs of science or the preachers of virtue—a heap of brute force and of low appetites, according to them—but rather as [matter] appears to me today, in [its] totality, and truth" (*HU*, p. 72 (69).

44. *HU*, p. 68 (65).

45. *DM*, p. 71 (45).

46. *Ibid.*, p. 108 (71); *HU*, p. 30 (30); *FoM*, p. 183 (144).

47. *PoM*, p. 137; see also *FoM*, pp. 75 (54f.), 124 (94).

48. *HU*, pp. 36 (36), 63 (61).

49. *DM*, p. 64 (41).

50. *HU*, p. 66 (64); *DM*, p. 107 (70).

51. *FoM*, p. 187 (147).

52. *HU*, p. 132 (123).

53. *DM*, p. 128 (86).

54. *Ibid.*, pp. 102 (67), 126 (84).

55. 1917, *HU*, p. 101f. (94).

56. *HU*, 166 (153). Note that this prayer, which neither asks for suffering nor pleads to be especially spared, thus avoids two unhealthy attitudes, imitating Jesus' prayer at Gethsemane (Matt. 26:39; Mark 14:36).

57. *HU*, p. 26 (27).

58. *DM*, p. 66 (42). Cf. Phil. 2:12f.: "Work out your own salvation with fear and trembling. For it is God which worketh in you. . . ."

59. *FoM*, p. 29 (17).

60. Cf. II Cor. 4:16: "So we do not lose heart. Though our outer nature is wasting away, our inner nature is being renewed every day. . . ."

61. *DM*, p. 94 (61).

62. Letter of 1916, *HU*, p. 163 (150). See *The Meaning and Constructive Value of Suffering* in Braybrooke, p. 26.

63. *HU*, pp. 130 (121f.), 140 (129f.); *DM*, pp. 93f. (61), 118f. (78).

64. Letter of 1919, cited in Cuénot, p. 47.

65. *DM*, p. 115f. (76).

66. *PoM*, p. 272.

67. *DM*, p. 89 (58).

68. *PoM*, p. 261.

69. *HU*, p. 130 (121).

70. Compare with the statement in *Doctrine in the Church of England* (1922; London: S.P.C.K., 1957), p. 202f., which shows the influence of William Temple: "The interest of most modern people in the 'Last Things' has an emphasis and perspective different from that disclosed in the New Testament. Today the predominant concern tends to be with the personal destiny of individuals. . . . That concern is indeed present in the New Testament (e.g., I Thess. 4:13-18), but it is subordinate. The predominant concern is with the fulfilment of the purpose of God—so manifestly not yet fulfilled on the historical plane. The destiny of the individual is a subordinate part of the whole purpose of God. We are convinced that if we are to think rightly in these matters we must recover the perspective of the New Testament: we must begin with the world-purpose of God, and must see everything else

in that context. The Gospel knows no private or merely individual salvation. . . . The world-purpose of God is wrought out partly through history; but for its complete and full working out it requires not only a 'new creation' of man, but a 'new earth' and 'new heavens.' "

We will discuss the fate of the nonbeliever in a later chapter.

71. See *DM*, p. 18 (12) and fn. to p. 29 (17).

72. *Ibid.*, p. 164 (111).

73. *FoM*, p. 96 (72).

74. *Ibid.*, p. 230 (183), and Rom. 7:23.

75. Nascent freedom, as in young children, seems to be naturally self-destructive unless exercised under authority. We need the law as our pedagogue until we become mature.

76. *FoM*, p. 31 (19), and Phil. 3:12f.; Col. 3:1-5.

77. *DM*, p. 29 (17) fn.

78. *HU*, p. 21 (21). Cf. Gal. 2:20, "It is no longer I who live, but Christ who lives in me, and the life I now live in the flesh I live by faith in the Son of God . . ." and I Cor. 10:17, "Let him who boasts, boast of the Lord."

79. Cf. Phil. 3:12.

80. *DM*, p. 153 (103).

81. *Ibid.*, p. 149 (101).

82. *HU*, p. 128 (119).

83. *DM*, p. 151 (102).

84. *HU*, p. 23 (24).

85. *DM*, p. 151 (102).

86. *Ibid.*, p. 155f. (105).

87. *HU*, p. 29 (30).

88. *Ibid.*, pp. 17ff. (19ff.).

89. *Ibid.*, p. 18 (20).

90. P. Smulders, p. 257. Father Henri de Lubac, p. 172, quotes from a memoir of Teilhard's: "Our work ultimately amounts to forming the host onto which the divine Fire is to fall." Here is Teilhard's view of history in a sentence.

91. *DM*, p. 154 (104).

CHAPTER 4: THE CHRISTIAN TRADITION

1. Cf. A. Richardson, p. 120: "Our modern difficulties about the relation of the Spirit to God arise because we hold a conception of personality unknown to the biblical writers. We think of separate and distinct personalities. . . . In the Bible . . . they flow into one another."

2. *Comment je vois*, Part II. See extracts in Crespy, p. 115f.

3. *PoM*, p. 31.

4. Witness the *filioque* clause in the Creed, which is still disputed between the Eastern and Western churches.

5. E.g., Rom. 8:9; II Cor. 3:17. For a fuller discussion see A. Richardson, pp. 120ff.

6. *Doctrine in the Church of England,* p. 95.

7. *DM,* p. 164 (111); John 6:44.

8. *DM,* p. 164 (112). The same dependence of all understanding on the spiritual gift of vision is expressed in a number of places without overtly invoking the Holy Spirit. See, e.g., the Foreword to *The Phenomenon of Man,* entitled "Seeing" (*PoM,* pp. 31ff.).

9. Teilhard also seems to be speaking of the action of the Holy Spirit under the designation of "la foi qui opère" (e.g., *HU,* pp. 142 [131], 149f. [138f.]; *DM,* p. 170 [115]), by which faith is given an active, quasi-personal role in the Christian's life.

10. *PoM,* pp. 309ff.

11. *Ibid.,* p. 309.

12. It is beyond our present scope to discuss the general question as to which of these approaches to Christian education is the better, either universally or in particular cases. It may be that one or the other is more effective in different circumstances or with people of different temperaments. It is worth noting, however, in the case of Kierkegaard, that if we look at his work as a whole series, he also uses a step by step method, leading men from the aesthetic, to the ethical, to the religious stage with its hope in "eternal happiness." And while Kierkegaard lays most stress on guilt and dread, Teilhard also trys to shock the humanist out of his ill-founded optimism.

13. Note that Teilhard does not rule out a fall (e.g., *PoM,* p. 311, *DM,* p. 117 [77]), but he relegates it to pretemporality, so that it has an ontological rather than an historical or phenomenological significance.

14. *PoM,* p. 310, and *Comment je vois,* cited in Crespy, p. 121.

15. *Comment je vois* (1948), cited and summarized in Crespy, Ch. V, and Smulders, Ch. VII. See also *HU,* p. 62 (60).

16. See *Summa Theologica,* Q. 48, Art. 3 and Q. 49, Art. 1,2.

17. *FoM,* p. 119 (90); italics mine.

18. *DM,* p. 188 (129).

19. Cited in H. de Lubac, p. 161.

20. *FoM,* pp. 179ff. (140).

21. *DM,* p. 86 (55).

22. See Rom. 12:12; Matt. 5:44, 7:1; John 12:47. See also the parable of the wheat and the tares, Matt. 13:24ff.

23. *FoM,* p. 183f. (144f.).

24. *The Meaning and Constructive Value of Suffering,* in

Braybrooke, p. 23. This highly personal essay is dedicated to Teilhard's sister, Marguerite-Marie, who was president of the Catholic Union for the Sick, and who died in 1936. She unfortunately destroyed almost all of her large correspondence with her brother. Another sister, Francoise, became the Mother Superior of the convent of the Little Sisters of the Poor in Shanghai, where she succumbed to smallpox at the age of thirty-two. See Cuénot, pp. 77, 170 and *LT,* p. 226. Also, *DM,* p. 87f. (56).

25. Braybrooke, p. 25.

26. *DM,* p. 89 (58).

27. *FoM,* p. 119 (90).

28. *DM,* p. 92 (60).

29. Braybrooke, p. 26.

30. *DM,* p. 18 (12).

31. *PoM,* p. 309.

32. It is interesting to see a Dominican Father suggesting that the theology of a Jesuit needs to be "supplemented and corrected by that of Barth" (Rabut, p. 209, fn.). See also Teilhard's own reference to "Barthian pessimism" (*LT,* p. 254).

33. Raven, p. 180.

34. Smulders, p. 165; see also Tresmontant, p. 95.

35. *LT,* p. 265, and *FoM,* p. 162 (127).

36. *LT,* pp. 57, 267; *HU,* p. 57 (54).

37. *HU,* p. 50f. (48f.).

38. The same thought is expressed by William Temple whose perspective is so similar to Teilhard's. "The value of an experience lasting through a period of time depends on its tendency and its conclusion, not upon the stages in isolation. . . . Though past facts cannot be altered their value can, so that the presence of evil in the world at any moment or through any period of time is not in principle any argument against the perfect goodness of the whole" (*Christus Veritas* [1922; London: Macmillan, 1962], p. 34).

39. *DM,* p. 90 (59); see also *HU,* p. 142 (132), and Rom. 8:28.

40. *DM,* p. 172 (117).

41. Frequently quoted by Teilhard from Léon Bloy, e.g., *LT,* p. 288.

42. *DM,* p. 188 (129).

43. *HU,* p. 142 (132); *DM,* p. 173 (118).

44. E.g., Smulders, p. 147; Crespy, p. 223.

45. *FoM,* p. 293 (227).

46. *La vision du passé,* p. 106. On the other hand, if our analysis of the relation between freedom, sin, and grace is correct, the danger that sin will increase in proportion to freedom is reduced by the

fact that growth in freedom depends more and more upon cooperation with grace as man ascends toward the goal. Refusal of grace leaves man in bondage and slows up the whole process of evolution toward greater freedom. The growth of freedom, on the other hand, cannot be said to limit God's omnipotence since it is God's own will that mankind be united to himself in love, a relationship which cannot be forced, by the very nature of things. In other words, it is God's own will that men should be free to choose between revolt and adoration.

47. *HU*, p. 50f. (48f.), and *DM*, p. 188 (129).

48. *PoM*, p. 287f.

49. *DM*, p. 188 (129), and *PoM*, p. 288.

50. *DM*, p. 187f. (128f.). We might note in passing that one of Crespy's principal criticisms of Teilhard is that he leaves no room for Christ as judge. "We have not found the slightest allusion in anything we have read of the Father's to the idea that God in Christ judges the world" (Crespy, p. 218). Yet Teilhard devotes five pages, 187-192 (128-131) of *DM* to the subject.

51. *DM*, p. 189 (129).

52. *HU*, p. 142 (132). Teilhard may well have the resource of purgatory in mind. If the purifying fires continue in some manner after death, then indeed, we may not judge until the end. And if the evil which a sinner does is converted by God through history into good, is it not possible that he may in some mysterious way win ultimately the sinner also?

53. *PoM*, pp. 276, 306f.

54. *FoM*, p. 305 (237).

55. Again the verses which appear on the last page of Father Teilhard's Journal (*FoM*, p. 404 [309]).

CHAPTER 5: CHRISTIANITY AND SOCIETY TODAY

1. A list of major sources would be either excessively long or highly arbitrary. They are, however, discussed in the following surveys with their bibliographies:

a. From a humanist standpoint:

R. G. Collingwood, *The Idea of History* (New York: Oxford University Press, 1946)

J. H. Randall, Jr., *The Making of the Modern Mind* (Boston: Houghton Mifflin Co., 1940)

b. From a Christian point of view:

M. C. D'Arcy, S.J., *The Meaning and Matter of History* (New York: Meridian Books, 1961)

Karl Löwith, *Meaning in History* (University of Chicago: Phoenix Books, 1949)

Alan Richardson, *History, Sacred and Profane* (Phila.: Westminster Press, 1964)

For a concise but thorough survey (with some existentialist bias) of the wide variety of theological attempts either to bridge the secular-theistic gap or to make a virtue of it, see John Macquarrie, *Twentieth-Century Religious Thought* (New York: Harper & Row, 1963).

2. See especially G. W. F. Hegel's introduction to his *The Philosophy of History,* trans. J. Sibree (New York: Dover Publications, 1956), and the discussions of Hegel and his followers in the works listed in note 1 above.

3. K. Löwith, p. 65.

4. E.g., *FoM,* pp. 242f. (191f.), 313 (241).

5. Before Teilhard, the movement for the Social Gospel, whose creed is expressed in Walter Rauschenbusch's *A Theology for the Social Gospel* (1917 [Nashville: Abingdon Press, 1945]), did pioneering work in relating the emerging historical interpretation of the Bible to the problems of the secular world. The catastrophes of the First World War and the Bolshevik Revolution, however, brought the Social Gospel into eclipse while neo-orthodox theology pointed up its weaknesses in respect to Grace, Christology, Ecclesiology, and Eschatology. It stands, nevertheless, as a brave preliminary sketch of the structure which Teilhard has filled out and founded on firmer theological and scientific grounds.

For a more recent effort to outline a biblical and theological basis for a social gospel and a "worldly Christianity," see J. A. T. Robinson, *On Being the Church in the World* (Phila.: Westminster Press, 1960).

6. Dietrich Bonhoeffer, *Letters and Papers from Prison* (London: S.C.M. Press, 1953), pp. 91ff. There are many close parallels between Teilhard's and Bonhoeffer's diagnosis and prescription for healing the "religious"-"worldly" rift. See especially Bonhoeffer's *Ethics* (New York: Macmillan, 1955), Chs. IV-VI. But Bonhoeffer, perhaps because of his early death at the hands of the Nazis, was never able fully to describe the place of worship and prayer in a "worldly Christianity." Teilhard was able to carry on well beyond where Bonhoeffer was so tragically cut off.

7. E.g., *FoM,* p. 105f. (80f.); *Le prêtre* in *HU,* p. 164 (151); Preface to *DM,* etc. In his introduction to *Comment je crois* (1934), Teilhard describes himself as one who was privileged to have been raised as a child of heaven and of earth at one and the same time.

Trained in the language and aspirations of two worlds usually considered as antagonistic, he raised no barriers between them but allowed both tendencies to interact freely in himself, and through the pursuit of inner unity discovered that a synthesis arose quite naturally between them.

8. *DM*, p. 64 (41); *HU*, p. 62f. (69f.).

9. Letter of Dec. 1936, Cuénot, p. 262.

10. *FoM*, p. 345 (265); *DM*, p. 97 (63).

11. E.g., *FoM*, p. 301 (234).

12. *Ibid.*, pp. 59 (39), 161 (126), 332 (255), etc.

13. *Ibid.*, p. 247 (193).

14. *Ibid.*, p. 330 (254).

15. *Ibid.*, p. 284 (222).

16. *Ibid.*, p. 325 (250).

17. In a letter of 1954, Teilhard observes, "During a symposium of three days (a closed meeting, seventy participants, almost all well-known and important people) which was held under the auspices of Columbia University . . . I was struck . . . that those who most refused to envisage the future possibility of an ultra-human reality on Earth were precisely the Christians (of all denominations)." Cuénot, p. 438f.

18. *FoM*, p. 331 (255).

19. *Ibid.*, p. 60 (40).

20. *Ibid.*, p. 314 (241). Teilhard does not make the all too common mistake of identifying Christianity with any existing political system or ideology. He both judges the abuses and finds value for future growth in certain aspects of democracy and Marxian socialism. Here, too, he would work for their reconciliation in a higher synthesis. *Ibid.*, pp. 242 (191), 313 (241), 343f. (263f.); Cuénot, p. 267.

21. *Ibid.*, p. 332 (256).

22. *Ibid.*, p. 74 (53).

23. *Ibid.*, p. 247f. (193f.).

24. *Ibid.*, p. 152 (119).

25. *Ibid.*, p. 283 (221).

26. *Ibid.*, p. 395 (303).

27. *Ibid.*, p. 99 (75).

28. *Ibid.*, p. 302f. (235f.).

29. *Ibid.*, pp. 63 (42), 173 (137).

30. *Ibid.*, p. 342 (263). In his First Epistle to the Corinthians, Saint Paul, speaking to those who boast of superior gifts of the spirit, shows them a "better way," the way of love. "So with yourselves;" he says, "since you are eager for manifestations of the Spirit, strive to excel in building up the church" (I Cor. 14:12). Is not Teilhard's whole thesis implicit in these words?

31. *FoM,* pp. 105f. (80), 345 (265); *Le Christique,* Cuénot, p. 452.

32. *FoM,* pp. 349 (269), 242 (192).

33. *Ibid.,* pp. 358 (274), 369 (283), 379 (291), 149 (117).

34. *Ibid.,* p. 164 (128).

35. *Ibid.,* p. 73 (52).

36. See especially, History and the Church (Ch. 2); Christ and the Individual (Ch. 3); Grace, the Church, and the Eucharist (Ch. 3).

37. *FoM,* p. 267 (208).

38. *HU,* p. 30 (31).

CHAPTER 6: TEILHARD'S METHODOLOGY

1. *Hu,* p. 67f. (64f.).

2. *PoM,* p. 29.

3. *FoM,* p. 161 (126).

4. *LT,* p. 86.

5. *PoM,* p. 289.

6. Elizabeth Sewell, *The Human Metaphor* (Univ. of Notre Dame Press, 1964), p. 26.

7. For a detailed discussion of the history and the effects of this stricture of thought and method on Western culture the reader is referred to the following books and their bibliographies:

Karl Löwith, *Meaning in History* (Univ. of Chicago Press, 1949)
M. C. D'Arcy, S.J., *The Meaning and Matter of History* (New York: Meridian, 1961)
Alan Richardson, *History, Sacred and Profane* (Phila.: Westminster Press, 1964)

8. I refer the reader to my principal sources and their bibliographies:

Michael Polanyi, *Personal Knowledge* (Univ. of Chicago Press, 1958)
Thomas S. Kuhn, *The Structure of Scientific Revolutions* (Univ. of Chicago Press, 1962). References are to Phoenix ed., 1964.
Herbert Butterfield, *The Origins of Modern Science* (New York: Collier, 1962)

9. Letter of 1954, cited in Cuénot, p. 482.

10. Kuhn, p. 10.

11. *HU,* p. 57 (54).

12. Kuhn, p. 43; Polanyi, pp. 70ff., 160ff.; *PoM,* p. 218.

13. Polanyi, p. 60.

14. *PoM,* p. 30.

15. Kuhn, p. 138.
16. *FoM*, p. 328 (252).
17. *Ibid.*, p. 79 (58).
18. Polanyi, p. 138.
19. Kuhn, pp. 121, 143.
20. Polanyi, p. 130.
21. *DM*, p. 159f. (108f.).
22. This also applies to falsification experiments designed by opponents of a proposed theory who must learn to think within its framework and rules before they can produce evidence which disputes its claims. No theory or faith can be disproven by evidence or arguments based on some other set of fundamental presuppositions.
23. Polanyi, p. 116.
24. *FoM*, p. 229 (181); cf. pp. 275 (214), 287 (225).
25. *PoM*, p. 32.
26. Polanyi, pp. 123ff.
27. E.g., the rules and axioms of traditional geometry are profoundly altered if transferred to a non-Euclidean space (or even from a plane to a spherical surface). The concept of the new space must be accepted before any of its implications make sense. Cf. *FoM*, p. 78f. (57f.).
28. Polanyi (p. 152) gives the example of how the craving to keep man at the center of the universe was the emotional force behind opposition to the Copernican theory. Opposition to Darwin's theory was similarly motivated.
29. Polanyi, pp. 151ff.
30. *FoM*, p. 334f. (257f.).
31. *PoM*, p. 30; see Polanyi, p. 255.
32. Polanyi, pp. 203ff.; *FoM*, pp. 260ff. (202ff.).
33. *FoM*, p. 262 (204).
34. Polanyi, p. 134.
35. *Ibid.*, pp. 275ff.; *PoM*, p. 232.
36. *FoM*, p. 100 (75).
37. *PoM*, p. 257.
38. Polanyi, p. 139f.
39. *PoM*, p. 219; *FoM*, p. 103 (78).
40. *PoM*, p. 53.
41. *Ibid.*, p. 189.
42. *Ibid.*, p. 248.
43. *FoM*, p. 79 (58); *PoM*, p. 30.
44. *FoM*, p. 241 (190).
45. *PoM*, pp. 54, 30.
46. For a survey and critique of recent work in this field, see:

Frederick Ferré, *Language, Logic and God* (New York: Harper & Row, 1961)

Austin Farrer, *The Glass of Vision* (Westminster: Dacre Press, 1948)

George Pitcher, *The Philosophy of Wittgenstein* (Englewood Cliffs: Prentice-Hall, 1964)

47. W. Heisenberg, M. Born, E. Schrödinger, P. Auger, *On Modern Physics* (New York: C. N. Potter, 1961), p. 19. This whole symposium is highly pertinent to our present discussion.

48. *Ibid.*, pp. 42, 53.

49. *PoM*, pp. 55ff.

50. Heisenberg *et al.*, pp. 90, 93.

51. *PoM*, p. 219f.; cf. *HU*, p. 81f. (77f.).

52. *FoM*, p. 202 (156); cf. *DM*, p. 43 (26).

53. Sewell, p. 85; Polanyi, pp. 15, 330ff., 353ff.

54. Polanyi, p. 39f.

55. *FoM*, pp. 268 (210), 118ff. (88ff.).

56. *PoM*, p. 228.

57. That is why Teilhard so frequently employs such words as "pre-life," "proto-consciousness," when he looks down the scale, and "hyper-personal" and "super-humanity" when he looks up.

58. *PoM*, p. 249; cf. *FoM*, pp. 262ff. (204ff.).

59. Cuénot, p. 452.

60. *DM*, p. 160f. (108f.).

61. *PoM*, pp. 284ff.

62. *HU*, p. 149f. (64f.); cf. pp. 22ff. (21ff.).

63. *DM*, p. 163 (111).

64. *Ibid.*, p. 25 (15); *PoM*, p. 232.

65. *DM*, p. 164 (112); cf. pp. 159ff. (108ff.).

66. *HU*, p. 129 (119).

Bibliography

I. BOOKS AND ANTHOLOGIES OF TEILHARD
DE CHARDIN'S WORK

Oeuvres, Paris: Editions du Seuil

I. *Le Phénomène Humain*, 1955
II. *L'Apparition de l'Homme*, 1956
III. *La Vision du Passé*, 1957
IV. *Le Milieu Divin*, 1957
V. *L'Avenir de l'Homme*, 1959
VI. *L'Energie Humaine*, 1962
VII. *L'Activation de l'Energie Humaine*, 1963

Hymne de l'Univers, 1961

American editions, New York: Harper & Row

The Phenomenon of Man, trans. B. Wall, 1959 (abbr. *PoM*)
The Divine Milieu, trans. B. Wall, 1960 (abbr. *DM*)
The Future of Man, trans. N. Denny, 1964 (abbr. *FoM*)
Hymn of the Universe, trans. S. Bartholemew, 1965 (abbr. *HU*)
The Appearance of Man, trans. J. M. Cohen, 1966

Other works

Le Groupe Zoologique Humain, Paris: Albin, 1956
Lettres de Voyage de 1923 à 1955, Paris: Grasset, 1961; English trans., *Letters from a Traveller*, New York: Harper & Row, 1962 (abbr. *LT*)
La Genèse d'une Pensée, Lettres de 1914 à 1919, Paris: Grasset, 1961

171

Unpublished writings

> *Comment je crois,* 1934
> *Esquisse d'un univers personnel,* 1936
> *Super-Humanité, Super-Christ, Super-Charité,* 1943
> *Comment je vois,* 1948
> *Le Christique,* 1955

II. OTHER BOOKS CITED

Bonhoeffer, Dietrich. *Letters and Papers from Prison.* London: S.C.M. Press, 1953.
——— *Ethics.* New York: Macmillan, 1955.
Braybrooke, Neville, ed. *Teilhard de Chardin, Pilgrim of the Future.* New York: Seabury Press, 1964.
Bultmann, Rudolf. *History and Eschatology.* New York: Harper & Bros., 1957.
Butterfield, Herbert. *The Origins of Modern Science.* New York: Collier Books, 1962.
Chastenet, Jacques. *Histoire de la Troisième République,* Vols. I-III. Paris: Hachette, 1960.
Collingwood, R. G. *The Idea of History.* New York: Oxford University Press, 1946.
Crespy, Georges. *La Pensée Théologique de Teilhard de Chardin.* Paris: Editions Universitaires, 1961.
Cuénot, Claude, *Pierre Teilhard de Chardin, Les Grandes Etapes de son Evolution.* Paris: Plon, 1958.
Cullmann, Oscar. *Christ and Time,* Philadelphia: Westminster Press, 1950.
D'Arcy, M. C. *The Meaning and Matter of History.* New York: Meridian Books, 1961.
Doctrine in the Church of England (1922). London: S.P.C.K., 1957.
Farrer, Austin. *The Glass of Vision.* Westminster: Dacre Press, 1948.
Ferré, Frederick. *Language, Logic and God.* New York: Harper & Row, 1961.
Francoeur, Robert T., ed. *The World of Teilhard de Chardin.* Baltimore: Helicon Press, 1961.
Hegel, G. W. F. *The Philosophy of History,* tr. J. Sibree. New York: Dover Publications, 1956.
Heisenberg, Werner, ET AL. *On Modern Physics.* New York: C. N. Potter, 1961.
Jacob, Edmond. *Theology of the Old Testament.* New York: Harper & Row, 1958.

Kuhn, Thomas S. *The Structure of Scientific Revolutions*. University of Chicago Press, 1962; Phoenix Books, 1964.

Löwith, Karl. *Meaning in History*. University of Chicago Press, Phoenix Books, 1949.

Lubac, Henri de. *La Pensée Religieuse du Père Teilhard de Chardin*. Paris: Aubier, 1962.

Macquarrie, John. *Twentieth-Century Religious Thought*. New York: Harper & Row, 1963.

Moule, C. F. D. *The Cambridge Greek Testament Commentary, Colossians*. Cambridge University Press, 1962.

Pitcher, George. *The Philosophy of Wittgenstein*. Englewood Cliffs: Prentice-Hall, 1964.

Polanyi, Michael. *Personal Knowledge*. University of Chicago Press, 1958.

Rabut, Olivier. *Teilhard de Chardin, A Critical Study*. New York: Sheed and Ward, 1961.

Randall, J. H., Jr. *The Making of the Modern Mind*. Boston: Houghton Mifflin, 1940.

Rauschenbusch, Walter. *A Theology for the Social Gospel*. Nashville: Abingdon Press, 1945.

Raven, Charles E. *Teilhard de Chardin, Scientist and Seer*. New York: Harper & Row, 1962.

Richardson, Alan. *An Introduction to the Theology of the New Testament*. New York: Harper & Row, 1958.

—— *History, Sacred and Profane*. Philadelphia: Westminster Press, 1964.

Robinson, J. A. T. *On Being the Church in the World*. Philadelphia: Westminster Press, 1960.

Sewell, Elizabeth. *The Human Metaphor*. University of Notre Dame Press, 1964.

Smulders, Pierre. *La Vision de Teilhard de Chardin*. Paris: Desclée de Brouwer, 1964.

Temple, William. *Nature, Man and God*. London: Macmillan, 1960.

—— *Christus Veritas*. London: Macmillan, 1962.

de Terra, Helmut. *Memories of Teilhard de Chardin*. New York: Harper & Row, 1964.

Tresmontant, Claude. *Pierre Teilhard de Chardin, His Thought*. Baltimore: Helicon Press, 1959.

INDEX OF KEY IDEAS